Business Communication and Cooperative Movement in Agriculture

Indian Council of
Agricultural Research (ICAR)

Dr. Balasaheb Sawant Konkan
Krishi Vidyapeeth (DBSKKV)

National Agricultural Higher Education
Project-Institutional Development Plan
(NAHEP-IDP)

NIPA® Genx Electronic Resources &
Solutions P. Ltd., New Delhi-110 034

About the Authors

Dr. Anita P Bobade, B.Com. MBA, PhD

Professor and I/ C Director, DES's Navinchandra Mehta Institute of Technology and Development, Mumbai

Dr. Anita Bobade, is a seasoned finance professional, having worked in Financial Service Sector, for more than 15 years with Institutions like UTI, IDBI Mutual Fund, Asit C Mehta, Sanmar Securities and Merchant Banking outfits. She joined Business School, later in life. Presently she is working as a Professor, MMS, with DES's Navinchandra Mehta Institute of Technology and Development and is in academics for 2 decades. Dr. Anita is an approved Professor and PhD guide of University of Mumbai. Dr. Anita Bobade, has been recently promoted as an I/C Director of DES NMITD. Dr. Anita is an established author, blogger and Financial Literacy Activist.

Recently she has authoured a book on Amazon, titled, " How You can Make a Million on the Stock Market" She has also translated this in Marathi, शेर मार्किट - तंत्र आणि मंत्र.

She is a B. Com of University of Mumbai, MBA from CSIBER and PhD from Leeds University, United Kingdom, in the area of Strategic Management. Dr. Anita is presently pursuing an interdisciplinary research, as a Post Doc Student of Oxford Center for Hindu Studies (OCHS) United Kingdom. The proposed title of the thesis is " Vedanta, Dharma and Management." Dr. Anita is also an approved PhD Guide for University of Mumbai in Management Studies.

Dr. Anita has authored over 32 research papers in peer reviewed journals and have 16 books, 32 research papers to her credit for under graduate and post graduate students of Management at University of Mumbai and two chapters in International books published by Palgrave Macmillan, U.K.

She is also a review for Scopus Based Inderscience Journal and International Journal of Business and Economics Research. Her areas of research interest: Strategic Management, Perspective Management, Financial Management and Financial Markets and Institution. Dr. Anita is nominated as a Country Director, for EuroMed Research & Business Institute, Switzerland since 2016 to promote their publications and conferences in India.

Her other notable achievements include, Member of the University of Mumbai, Sesquicentennial Committee, which published a souvenir which is a rare and unique collection of Art and Literature, applauded by the then President of India, His Excellency, Hon. Dr. APJ Kalam.

Dr. Anita is the recipient of Global Digital Teacher Award in November 2020, given by Global Digital Academy for the Ongoing Dedication of Impacting Excellence

Through the Development And Dissemination of Radically Transforming Learning Spectrum during Covid Pandemic 2019, through her online certifications and webinars for students and housewives to spread financial literacy called, " Dhan Ki Baat".

Dr. Anita Bobade's Social media handles:

https://www.linkedin.com/in/dr-anita-bobade-08639811/

https://www.researchgate.net/profile/Anita-Bobade/savedlist

http://dranitabobade.com/

https://www.amazon.in/dp/B092ZDMKCB

https://www.amazon.in/dp/B08LPN4WQD

https://indianethosinmanagement.wordpress.com/

https://www.youtube.com/channel/UC-9K64MsSPxnvcIfTHbQPKg

https://www.facebook.com/anita.bobade.144/

Shri Chintan Oza, Founder, Anantam Ecosystems, Regional Director, Founder Institute, Member, IISEC at IEEE TEMS, India Region Lead at IEEE Entrepreneurship

Chintan is a serial entrepreneur with 23 years of experience in the telecom and ICT sectors. He is an alumnus of IIT Mumbai, UC Berkeley, and Oxford University, and holds a certification in Innovation and Technology Commercialization from Georgia Tech.

Chintan is currently the local leader of the Founder Institute in Mumbai and the Regional Director for India. He has worked with over 380 entrepreneurs across six continents, helping them with go-to-market strategies and scaling up their technology.

Chintan is also an active volunteer at several organizations, including the Project Management Institute, IEEE Technology Engineering Management Society, IEEE Entrepreneurship, Bombay Management Association, OneQuantum, Emerging Technologies Forum, Stanford Seed, Indian Chamber of International Business, and Rotary International.

He is on the advisory boards of several startups and academic institutions, and he has been an angel investor in three startups. He is also part of the investment committee for various venture capital funds, and collaborates with investment syndicates and angel investors. He is also an adjunct faculty member and a member of the advisory board at various academic institutions.

Chintan co-founded Arnima Energy Solutions, which is gearing up to launch a range of electric vehicles and high-speed chargers. He is also the India Region Lead for IEEE Entrepreneurship and is organizing a series of virtual events on the theme of protecting innovation.

Chintan is a member of the Council for Alliance Task Force at Startup20, a newly formed engagement group within the G20 under India's presidency in 2023.

In July 2023, Chintan gave a talk on the leadership imperatives for transformation in business and social practices for a sustainable future at the Sustainable Business and Climate Change Summit, organized by the Consulate General of the United Arab Emirates in Mumbai. This was a side event of COP28, which will be held in the UAE in 2023.

You can reach Chintan on LinkedIn.

https://www.linkedin.com/in/chintanoza/

Dr. Kasturi R Naik, Assistant Professor, Sparsh Global Business School| Author | HRBP 2.0 Practitioner | NLP Practitioner | L & D Consultant | Life Coach Specialized in Emotional Intelligence, Email: kasturi.rnaik@sparshgbs.in

Link to follow: https://scholar.google.com/citations?user=kXaoxq0AAAAJ

Dr. Kasturi R Naik is known for real-time, forthright, solutions to complex people's problems. Knows the difference between Passion, Profession, and Purpose and that has made all the difference to the way she lives her life. She has more than 12 years of academic experience and 5 years of consultancy experience in the fields of human resource management, leadership, and team building for various corporate, educational institutions, and NGOs. At present, she is associated as an Assistant Professor with Sparsh Global Business School. She has been associated as a visiting faculty at JBIMS and GNIMS for MHRD and e-MBA courses and a resource person at XLRI and IIBF. She has also been associated with VMENTOR.ai as a mentor and subject matter expert in the domain of human resource management. Dr. Kasturi R Naik is the recipient of multiple national and international awards and accolades for her enriching work in the field of emotional intelligence, personality enhancement, stress management, and leadership development.

Her credentials include Ph.D. with Stress management as a broad area of research, MMS, BPHARM, DLL, Internationally Certified & Licensed Heal Your Life Workshop Leader and Life Coach, Certified in Positive Psychology: Resilience Skills, Certified in Building Your Leadership Skills by HEC Paris, Certified Executive Life Coach, Certified Image Consultant, Certified Emotional Intelligence Practitioner, Certified NLP Practitioner, and HRBP 2.0 Practitioner. Her research capabilities are self-proven through the 30+ research papers that she has published nationally and internationally, out of which she got the best paper awards in a couple of conferences as well and published in the ABDC category journal.

Dr. Kasturi R Naik has also been honored to play a role of the discussant and session chair in national and international conferences and has also won Best Paper track presenter award at ABRM International conference 2015, besides Best paper award at IMRC 2016.

Areas of Research & Consultancy Interest:

Leadership Ecosystem Development

Strategic HR Partnering, and

Learning and Development

Business Communication and Cooperative Movement in Agriculture

Compiled by

Prashant S. Bodake, Dean & Director of Instruction, DBSKKV
Co-ordinator & Principal Investigator, NAHEP-IDP, DBSKKV, Dapoli

Srinivasan Iyengar, Director of Jamnalal Bajaj Institute of Management Studies, Mumbai, Maharashtra

S.R.Torane, Deputy Director of Research
In-Charge PME Cell,DBSKKV-Dapoli, Maharashtra

Authors

Anita Bobade, Professor, DES Navinchandra Mehta Institute of Technology & Development, Dadar-Mumbai

Chintan Oza, Founder, Anantam Ecosystems

Kasturi Naik, Head &Assistant Professor, Sparsh Global Business School
Greater Noida, Delhi

Indian Council of Agricultural Research (ICAR)

Dr. Balasaheb Sawant Konkan Krishi Vidyapeeth (DBSKKV)

National Agricultural Higher Education Project-Institutional Development Plan (NAHEP-IDP)

NIPA® Genx Electronic Resources & Solutions P. Ltd., New Delhi-110 034

Citation: National Agriculture Higher Education Project Institutional Development Plan, DBSKKV, Dapoli & ICAR, New Delhi

NIPA® GENX ELECTRONIC RESOURCES & SOLUTIONS P. LTD.

101,103, Vikas Surya Plaza, CU Block
L.S.C.Market, Pitam Pura, New Delhi-110 034
Ph : +91 11 27341616, 27341717, 27341718
E-mail: newindiapublishingagency@gmail.com
Website: www.nipabooks.com

For customer assistance, please contact
Phone: + 91-11-27 34 17 17
Fax: + 91-11-27 34 16 16

ISBN: 978-93-58871-00-5

Composed and Designed by NIPA®.

भारतीय कृषि अनुसंधान परिषद
कृषि अनुसंधान भवन-II, नई दिल्ली-110012
INDIAN COUNCIL OF AGRICULTURAL RESEARCH
KRISHI ANUSANDHAN BHAVAN-II, PUSA, NEW DELHI-110012
Phone: +91-11-25841760
Email: ddg.edu@icar.gov.in, ddgedn@gmail.com, nd.nahep@icar.gov.in

Dr. Rakesh Chandra Agrawal
Deputy Director General (Agril. Edn.)

Message

It is with immense pleasure and a sense of purpose that I provide this forward to the National Agricultural Higher Education Project-Institutional Development Plan (NAHEP-IDP) at Dr. Balasaheb Sawant Konkan Krishi Vidyapeeth (DBSKKV) and the concurrent endeavour to develop a short pilot course in skilling small-scale agri-entrepreneurship. This transformative initiative is under the guidance and leadership of the Hon'ble Vice Chancellor of DBSKKV Dr.S.G.Bhave.

Principal Investigator of NAHEP-IDP, DBSKKV-Dapoli Dr. P.S.Bodake, a distinguished and visionary leader in the field of agriculture, has consistently championed the cause of advancing agricultural education, research, and extension services. His strategic vision has played a pivotal role in shaping the trajectory of agricultural development in our nation, with a keen focus on empowering farming communities and fostering innovation.

The NAHEP-IDP of DBSKKV stands as a testament to ICAR & World Bank commitment to elevating the standards of agricultural education. By providing institutional support and promoting excellence across various facets of academia, research, and extension activities, the project aims to position DBSKKV as a center of excellence in agricultural learning and research.

In tandem with the NAHEP-IDP, the initiation of a short pilot course in skilling smallscale agri-entrepreneurship reflects DBSKKV foresight in addressing contemporary challenges in agriculture. Recognizing the pivotal role played by small-scale agri-entrepreneurs in driving rural economies, this course is designed to equip them with the necessary skills and knowledge to navigate the dynamic landscape of agribusiness.

The NAHEP-IDP, DBSKKV envisions this pilot course as a stepping stone toward fostering a culture of entrepreneurship in agriculture. By blending theoretical insights with practical applications, the course seeks to empower agri-entrepreneurs, enabling them to adopt sustainable farming practices, embrace innovation, and contribute significantly to the economic prosperity of their communities.

I extend my heartfelt appreciation to Dr. P.S. Bodake and his entire NAHEP-IDP Team for their steadfast leadership and unwavering commitment to advancing agricultural education and entrepreneurship. Under his guidance, these initiatives are poised to make a lasting impact on the agricultural education landscape and the entrepreneurial spirit within the students and farming community.

(R.C. Agrawal)
Deputy Director General (Agril. Edn.)

DR. BALASAHEB SAWANT KONKAN KRISHI VIDYAPEETH
Dapoli, Dist. Ratnagiri - 415712
Tel. No.: (0)02358-282064, **Fax No.**: 02358-282074, **Mob.**: 9422556565
E-mail : vcdbskkv-mh@gov.in, ipmbhave@gmail.com, **website** : www.dbskkv.org

Dr. Sanjay G. Bhave
IDP Leader
Vice Chancellor, DBSKKV

Message

I am delighted to present the Institutional Development Plan as part of the National Agricultural Higher Education Project (NAHEP) undertaken by our esteemed institution. This initiative marks a significant milestone in our commitment to advancing agricultural education, research, and innovation, with the ultimate goal of transforming the agricultural landscape of our nation.

This pilot course serves as a testament to our university's dedication to fostering innovation and fostering collaboration between academia and industry. We believe that by offering this course, we are not only contributing to the skill development of individuals but also playing a pivotal role in shaping the future of agriculture.

We, at DBSKKV are happy to felicitate the proficient attainment of the Principal Investigator, IDP Coordinator, and Dean and Director of Instruction of DBSKKV-Dr.Prashant S. Bodake and team NAHEP-IDP involved in the same vertical. Your magnificent work makes all of us highly gratified and prosperous. Well Done!

I extend my gratitude to the faculty members, industry experts, and stakeholders who have contributed their expertise and insights to the development of this course. Their collective efforts have ensured that the curriculum aligns with the ever-changing demands of the agricultural sector.

I am excited to witness the impact that this short pilot course on skilling small-scale agricultural entrepreneurship will have on our participants and, consequently, on the agricultural landscape. With this initiative, we are sowing the seeds of empowerment and innovation, cultivating a new generation of agripreneurs who will not only navigate challenges but also unearth opportunities for growth.

(Sanjay G. Bhave)
IDP Leader
Vice Chancellor, DBSKKV

NATIONAL AGRICULTURAL HIGHER EDUCATION PROJECT
AGRICULTURAL EDUCATION DIVISION
INDIAN COUNCIL OF AGRICULTURAL RESEARCH
(Department of Agricultural Research and Education
Ministry of Agriculture and Farmers Welfare, Government of India)
Room No. 514, Krishi Anusandhan Bhawan-II, Pusa, New Delhi-110 012

Date : 14.12.2023

Dr. N.K. Jain
National Coordinator (IDP)

Message

It is a matter of great pleasure to learn that Dr. Balasaheb Sawant Konkan Krishi Vidyapeeth, Dapoli has developed short pilot course on "Skilling Small-scale Agri-Entrepreneurship" for the undergraduate students. The efforts made by DBSKKV, Dapoli and the Knowledge Experts is a significant stride towards fostering interdisciplinary learning and preparing students for the evolving landscape of agriculture. Agriculture, the backbone of our nation, is undergoing a transformative phase that demands a comprehensive understanding of not only traditional farming practices but also entrepreneurial skills. In this context, DBSKKV, Dapoli is driven by the vision to equip undergraduate students with the knowledge and skills necessary to navigate the complexities of modern agriculture and contribute to the burgeoning field of agri-entrepreneurship. I commend the leadership of Dr. S.G. Bhave, Hon'ble Vice Chancellor, DBSKVV, Dapoli for his forward-thinking approach in embracing this initiative and commitment to provide a robust academic environment aligns seamlessly with our objective of preparing students for the dynamic and competitive landscape of agriculture and entrepreneurship.

I also congratulate Dr. P.S. Bodake, Principal Investigator of NAHEP-IDP, DBSKKV, Dapoli and his entire team, whose collaborative efforts have been instrumental in shaping the curriculum of this course. Together, we envision a program that not only imparts knowledge but also nurtures a spirit of inquiry and enterprise among the students. I extend my warmest congratulations to the University on the launch of the innovative short pilot course on "Skilling Small-scale Agri-Entrepreneurship". May this endeavour be a beacon of progress, fostering excellence in agricultural education and empowering the next generation of agri-entrepreneurs. University's commitment to bridging theory and practical is commendable, and I am confident that this initiative will contribute significantly to the growth of our agricultural landscape.

Place: New Delhi

(N. K. Jain)

NAHEP THE WORLD BANK

NATIONAL AGRICULTURE HIGHER EDUCATION PROJECT INSTITUTIONAL DEVELOPMENT PLAN

DR. BALASAHEB SAWANT KONKAN KRISHI VIDYAPEETH,

DAPOLI, DIST. RATNAGIRI

Mob. No.: 9420413255 / 8275201130

Email.: (P)prameghash@gmail.com (O) hodagrodapoli@gmail.com (O) piidpdbskkv@gmail.com (O)nodalcelldbskkv@gmail.com

Dr. P. S. Bodake
Dean & Director of Instruction
Coordinator, Principal Investigator, NAHEP-IDP

Message

It is with immense pride and anticipation that I present the Institutional Development Plan as part of our active involvement in the National Agricultural Higher Education Project (NAHEP). This plan embodies our institution's unwavering commitment to redefining agricultural education and research, and it signifies a transformative journey towards excellence and innovation.

Through this plan, we aim to enhance our institutional capacities, bolster research initiatives, and cultivate strategic partnerships with industries and communities. By incorporating modern pedagogical techniques, fostering interdisciplinary collaboration, and harnessing the potential of emerging technologies, we strive to create a learning ecosystem that empowers our students to become leaders and change-makers in the agricultural sector and it will not only elevate our institution's stature but also propel the agricultural education and research landscape towards a brighter and more sustainable future.

Our joint commitment to education and empowerment has culminated in the creation of this pilot course. Through a harmonious blend of theoretical insights and practical experiences, participants will delve into market trends, value chain analysis, sustainable practices, financial management, and the integration of technology into agriculture. This holistic approach is designed to prepare individuals to navigate the intricacies of agripreneurship with confidence.

This pilot course is an embodiment of our dedication to fostering collaboration between academia and industry. By bridging the gap between theory and practice, we aim to nurture a new generation of agripreneurs who are poised to steer the agricultural sector towards innovation and growth.

We sincerely mention primitive gratitude towards the former Vice-chancellor of DBSKKV Dr. Sanjay D. Sawant and also present Vice-chancellor of DBSKKV Dr. Sanjay G. Bhave for their prudent leadership and providence. We feel proud to highlight the sheer hard work and great dedication of the Co-Principal Investigator of NAHEP-IDP and IDP Staff.

We are grateful to the Director of Jamnalal Bajaj Institute of Management-Mumbai Dr. Shrinivasan Iyengar for such excellent association and cordial congruence in the course of developing a short pilot course in skilling small-scale Agri-Entrepreneurship. We also express our sincere gratitude to the faculty members of JBIMS & University of Mumbai, industry experts, and stakeholders whose expertise and contributions have shaped this course. Their collective wisdom ensures that the curriculum remains attuned to the evolving demands of the agricultural landscape.

Thank you.

(P. S. Bodake)
Dean & Director of Instruction
Coordinator, Principal Investigator, NAHEP-IDP

Preface I

"Your ability to communicate with others, will account for 85% of your success in business and in life"

– Brian Tracey

The main objective of the Course is to transform and modernize agricultural education to produce globally competitive and skilled human resources for the agricultural sector and one of the course offered is Business Skills. For students pursuing agriculture or allied business, the Business Skills course becomes highly significant. Agricultural education is rapidly evolving to meet the needs of rural communities in India, This course focuses on essential business skills such as Business Communication, Entrepreneurship Development, knowledge of the latest Government schemes to enhance business opportunities, and an understanding of the global and Indian Cooperative Movement.

These modules aim to raise students' awareness and provide them with the necessary tools to create sustainable and profitable business ventures. The first module, Business Communication, is recognized worldwide as the key to economic development and overall progress. It covers the importance of communication in agriculture, communication strategies for successful agribusiness, the impact of Covid-19 on the agribusiness value chain, and effective utilization of social media and e-business strategies, including crisis management.

The second module delves into entrepreneurship in agribusiness, covering different types of entrepreneurs, required skills, current trends in the industry, and emerging technologies. It also highlights various government schemes promoting agricultural and allied business, emphasizing the need to familiarize students with entrepreneurship development concepts, methodologies, techniques, and supporting organizations.

The final module focuses on the evolution of the cooperative movement globally and in India. It introduces cooperative societies as a form of organization, explaining their scope, organizational structure, and the significance of the International Cooperative Alliance. Case studies are included to showcase successful cooperative movements both in India and abroad.

Agriculture and allied business in rural areas offer limitless opportunities for those passionate about success. This course equips students with fundamental business communication skills, entrepreneurship knowledge, and the essentials of forming cooperative societies, enabling them to be prepared for the world of business.

Authors

Preface II

"If you really look closely, most overnight successes took a long time."

– Steve Jobs

In the world of business, as in nature, success often appears like an overnight phenomenon. However, upon closer examination, one realizes that most triumphant ventures have actually been years in the making. Like a towering tree that reaches the skies, the true foundation of achievement lies hidden beneath the surface. Just as roots tirelessly dig through the solid ground to stabilize and nourish the tree's growth, business skills are honed through persistence, dedication, and a continuous journey of learning and adaptation. This preface explores the unseen but vital elements that contribute to the growth and prosperity of businesses, shedding light on the enduring efforts that pave the way for remarkable success.

This comprehensive course on " Business Skills" is designed to equip students with essential skills and knowledge to excel in the dynamic and evolving world of agriculture and agribusiness. In today's global economy, agribusiness plays a vital role in providing food security, rural development, and economic growth. As such, it demands individuals with a unique set of competencies, combining business acumen with a deep understanding of the agricultural sector.

The modules covered in this course have been thoughtfully curated to provide students with a holistic learning experience. Throughout this journey, we will delve into key areas such as Effective Communication, Entrepreneurship and Self-Help Groups, Social Entrepreneurship, and the concept of Co-operation and the Co-operative Movement, focusing on its rise in India and its impact globally.

Module 1: Understanding Business Communication Strategies and Techniques in Agricultural Context

This module has focused on providing readers with a comprehensive understanding of business communication strategies and techniques in the Indian agricultural context. The module has highlighted the importance of communication in business, the challenges faced by the agricultural sector in India, and the need for effective communication strategies to overcome these challenges. The module has also provided an overview of relevant communication theories and techniques and their application in the Indian agricultural context. Understanding business communication is critical to developing effective marketing, supply chain, and other business-related strategies in the Indian agricultural context, and this module has laid a strong foundation for the same.

Module 2: Entrepreneurship and Self-Help Groups and Helpful Information regarding various Government Schemes for Agri and Allied Business

The agribusiness sector offers immense opportunities for entrepreneurs to innovate, add value, and drive growth. This module will introduce students to the principles of entrepreneurship, encouraging them to think creatively and critically about agribusiness ventures. Additionally, we will explore the concept of Self-Help Groups (SHGs) as a powerful tool for empowering rural communities and fostering inclusive development.

This module also covers Social Entrepreneurship. In an era where social and environmental responsibilities are paramount, the importance of social entrepreneurship cannot be overstated. This module will introduce students to the concept of social entrepreneurship in the context of agribusiness. By examining successful social enterprises, students will gain inspiration and insights into creating sustainable business models that benefit both society and the environment.

Module 3: Co-operation and the Co-operative Movement

The cooperative movement has emerged as a transformative force, bringing farmers and producers together to achieve common goals. In this module, we will sensitize students to the concept of co-operation, its historical significance, and its global impact. We will also examine the rise of the cooperative movement in India and its influence on the country's agricultural landscape.

Throughout this course, students will read about real- life case studies, interactive discussions, and practical questions, which would bridge the gap between theory and practice. The aim is to empower students with the necessary skill set to navigate the challenges and opportunities in the agribusiness sector confidently.

We hope this course will serve as a catalyst for personal and professional growth, enabling students to contribute meaningfully to the sustainable development of agribusiness and the welfare of agricultural communities. Let's embark on this enriching journey together as we explore the new course of Business Skills for Agribusiness.

Authors

Contents

Summary

Summary of the Module: Business Communication

Business communication plays a crucial role in the education and development of Agri and Allied business students in India. Here are the key reasons highlighting the importance of business communication for these students.

Effective Collaboration: Agri and Allied businesses involve multiple stakeholders, including farmers, suppliers, distributors, and consumers. Clear and efficient communication is essential to establish effective collaborations among these diverse groups. Students with strong business communication skills can facilitate seamless interactions and build mutually beneficial relationships. Market Understanding: Agri and Allied business students need to comprehend market trends, consumer preferences, and industry dynamics. Communication skills enable them to gather and interpret information effectively, such as conducting market research, understanding customer feedback, and analyzing industry reports. This knowledge helps them make informed business decisions and adapt their strategies accordingly. Negotiation and Persuasion: Successful business transactions often require negotiation and persuasion skills. Agri and Allied business students must negotiate contracts, pricing, and terms with suppliers, buyers, and other business partners. Effective communication empowers students to articulate their ideas persuasively, present compelling arguments, and reach mutually beneficial agreements.

Branding and Marketing: Strong communication skills are indispensable for promoting and marketing agricultural products and services. Agri and Allied business students need to convey their brand's message, differentiate themselves from competitors, and create a positive image in the market. Effective communication techniques such as advertising, public relations, and social media marketing are vital to building a strong brand presence.

Professional Networking: Networking plays a significant role in the Agri and Allied industries. Building professional relationships with industry experts, potential investors, and other stakeholders can open doors to new opportunities. Effective business communication skills help students establish meaningful connections, communicate their goals and aspirations, and create a positive impression within the industry. Leadership and Teamwork: Agri and Allied business students often work in teams, requiring effective communication for collaboration and leadership. They must convey their ideas, delegate tasks, provide feedback, and motivate team members. Strong communication skills enable students to lead effectively, foster teamwork, and achieve collective goals.

The COVID-19 pandemic has had a significant impact on the agribusiness value chain. Here are some key implications, Production, Supply Chain and Logistics and market volativility. To mitigate these challenges, agribusinesses implemented strategies such as diversifying markets, adopting digital technologies for remote work and communication, implementing safety protocols to protect workers, and exploring alternative distribution channels. Collaboration among stakeholders, including farmers, suppliers, distributors, and governments, was crucial in addressing the disruptions and maintaining a functioning agribusiness value chain. It also used crisis communication strategies to engage with various stakeholders. Social media played a vital role in agribusiness communication during the COVID-19 pandemic.

In summary, business communication is of utmost importance for Agri and Allied business students in India. It facilitates collaboration, market understanding, negotiation, branding, problem-solving, networking, and leadership. Developing and honing these skills equips students to excel in the dynamic and competitive Agri and Allied sectors, contributing to their personal growth and the overall success of their businesses.

Summary of the Module : Co-operatives

This module would provide students with a comprehensive understanding of the Cooperative Society form of organization. Firstly, students will acquire a basic understanding of how Cooperative Societies operate and the principles they adhere to. This will include learning about the cooperative structure, decision-making processes, and the benefits of collective ownership and democratic control.

Secondly, students will explore the evolution and history of the Cooperative form of organization. They will delve into the origins of cooperatives, their growth and how the socio-economic factors have influenced their growth. Understanding the historical context will enable students to appreciate the importance of cooperatives in addressing social and economic challenges.

Thirdly, the module aims to sensitize students to the progress of the Cooperative Movement globally. They will examine successful cooperative models and case studies from different countries, gaining insights into the diverse sectors where cooperatives thrive. This global perspective will help students appreciate the versatility and potential of the cooperative model in different cultural and economic contexts.

The students are also acquainted with the International Co-operative Alliance (ICA) and its pivotal role in the development of the Cooperative movement worldwide. They will learn about the ICA's functions, initiatives, and advocacy efforts in promoting cooperative values, principles, and best practices on a global scale. Recognizing the significance of the ICA will enable students to understand how cooperative societies collaborate and share knowledge internationally.

The module also traces the history of the Co-operative Movement in India, before and after Independence. The different types of Co-operatives and its role in the economic and social development of rural India. It also discusses the legislative framework governing Co-operatives in India. It also makes a mention of SHG and its importance in rural economy. Many Case Studies of Successful Co-operatives are also discussed in the Module.

Overall, this course aims to equip students with a comprehensive understanding of Cooperative Societies, their historical development, global progress, and the vital role played by the International Co-operative Alliance in advancing the cooperative movement globally.

Summary of the Module : Entrepreneurship

The students are introduced to the concept and Overview of Entrepreneurship: Entrepreneurship refers to the process of identifying and creating new business opportunities, organizing resources, and taking risks to start and manage a business venture. Entrepreneurs are individuals who possess innovative ideas, take calculated risks, and bring about economic and social change through their ventures. They are driven by a desire for independence, the pursuit of opportunities, and the willingness to bear uncertainties and challenges.

The chapter also deals with the following , Need for and Importance of Entrepreneurship in Agriculture and Allied Industries: The crucial role it plays in agriculture and allied industries for introducing Innovation and Technology,

Environmental Sustainability: Entrepreneurial initiatives in agriculture promote sustainable practices, conservation of natural resources, and climate change mitigation.

It also documents the Government schemes and incentives for promotion of entrepreneurship: Various governments around the world have implemented schemes and incentives to promote entrepreneurship. These initiatives aim to foster innovation, create job opportunities, and support the growth of small and medium-sized enterprises. Some common examples include tax benefits, grants, loans, mentorship programs, and incubation centers. These schemes are designed to provide financial and non-financial assistance to entrepreneurs and startups.

The chapter also documents focus on agriculture in G20 countries under India's Presidency in 2023: As India holds the Presidency of the G20 in 2023, it is likely to prioritize discussions and initiatives related to agriculture. The focus may include promoting sustainable agricultural practices, addressing food security challenges, facilitating agricultural trade, and encouraging technological innovation in the sector. Through collaborative efforts and policy discussions, G20 countries may work towards creating an enabling environment for agricultural startups and entrepreneurs. It also elaborates the role of venture capital investments: Venture capital (VC) plays a crucial role in supporting entrepreneurship and startup ecosystems.

1

Understanding Business Communication Strategies and Techniques in India Agricultural Context

Learning objectives

1-1 To identify the importance of business communication in the agricultural sector.

1-2 To define different communication channels and evaluate their effectiveness in business communication.

1-3 To evaluate the role of effective communication strategies in promoting successful agricultural business outcomes.

1-4 To develop effective business communication messages for a given stakeholder audience.

1-5 To evaluate the role of different types of reports in communicating essential information within an Indian agricultural context.

1-6 To develop effective communication strategies in an agricultural context, using examples of best practices and case studies.

This chapter has focused on providing readers with a comprehensive understanding of business communication strategies and techniques in the Indian agricultural context. The chapter has highlighted the importance of communication in business, the challenges faced by the agricultural sector in India, and the need for effective communication strategies to overcome these challenges. The chapter has also provided an overview of relevant communication theories and techniques and their application in the Indian agricultural context. Understanding business communication is critical to developing effective marketing, supply chain, and other business-related strategies in the Indian agricultural context, and this chapter has laid a strong foundation for the same.

1.1 Definition of business communication and its role in agriculture communication

Business communication can be defined as the exchange of information and ideas within and between organizations to achieve a specific goal or objective. It encompasses all types of communication, including written, oral, and non-verbal communication. Effective communication is essential for the success of any business, and the same is true for agriculture in India. The importance of effective business communication in the Indian agricultural context, with special emphasis on the cooperative model, cannot be overstated.

Indian agriculture is characterized by small and fragmented land holdings, low productivity, and a lack of modern technology and infrastructure. To overcome these challenges, the cooperative model has emerged as one of the most effective ways to promote agricultural growth. A cooperative is a voluntary organization owned and controlled by its members, based on the principle of mutual self-help. It is a democratic institution that provides a variety of services to its members, including credit, inputs, marketing, and processing facilities.

In the Indian agricultural context, communication is central to the functioning of cooperatives. The cooperative model depends on effective communication between members, management, and other stakeholders to achieve its objectives. Communication plays a crucial role in the following areas:

1. Marketing: Cooperatives play a significant role in marketing agricultural produce. Effective communication is necessary to gain market access and to negotiate fair prices for farmers. Without effective communication, the cooperative may not be able to identify market opportunities, develop marketing strategies, or build relationships with buyers.
2. Input supply: Cooperatives can provide farmers with various inputs such as seeds, fertilizers, and pesticides at reasonable prices. Effective communication is essential to ensure that the members are aware of the availability and quality of input supplies, the terms and conditions of purchase, and the pricing policy.
3. Credit: Cooperatives can provide credit to members at affordable rates of interest. Effective communication is essential to ensure that members are aware of the credit policies, the terms and conditions of borrowing, and the repayment schedule.
4. Processing and value addition: Cooperatives can provide facilities for processing and value addition of agricultural produce. Effective communication is essential to ensure that members are aware of the

processing facilities and the quality standards that need to be met to access these facilities.

5. Capacity building: Cooperatives can provide training and capacity-building programs to members. Effective communication is essential to ensure that members are aware of the training programs, their objectives, and the eligibility criteria.

In the Indian agricultural context, where literacy levels improved and various options of communications have opened up which facitilitates for better communication. The communication method includes:

1. Use of local dialects: Cooperatives have used local dialects to communicate with members who are not proficient in the official language.
2. Use of visual aids: Cooperatives have used pictures, charts, and diagrams to explain complex concepts and ideas.
3. Use of mobile technology: Many cooperatives make use of mobile technology to communicate with members. Mobile phones are widely used in rural India through SMS, voice calls, and mobile apps to reach out to members.
4. Use of social media: Cooperatives have used social media platforms like WhatsApp and Facebook to communicate with members, share information, and conduct online meetings.

Effective communication plays a crucial role in the functioning of cooperatives in the Indian agricultural context. Cooperatives depend on effective communication to achieve their objectives of marketing, input supply, credit, processing and value addition, and capacity building. Innovative methods such as using local dialects, visual aids, mobile technology, and social media have been used by cooperatives to overcome the challenges of effective communication. As India strives to achieve agricultural growth, effective business communication will continue to be an essential ingredient of success.

1.2 Overview of different types of communication channels and media used in business communication

Communication is an essential component of business activities, including agriculture. In India, agriculture remains an important sector of the economy, and communication plays a significant role in promoting the industry's growth and competitiveness. This part provides an overview of the different types of communication channels and media used in business communication in the agricultural context in India, along with real examples.

Face-to-face communication is one of the most important communication channels used in the agricultural industry in India. It involves direct interaction between individuals and is widely used by farmers, traders, and suppliers. For example, face-to-face communication is used during field visits and office meetings, where farmers can discuss crop management techniques, fertilizers, and irrigation issues with agricultural extension workers, who can help provide solutions to the issues. Face-to-face communication is critical in promoting trust and building long-lasting relationships between different stakeholders in the agricultural industry in India. (Maulik & Debnath, 2013)

Electronic communication is another important communication channel used in the agricultural industry in India. It includes various digital channels like emails, messaging apps, and social media, among others. Electronic communication has revolutionized agriculture communication in India by providing farmers access to market information, enabling them to sell their produce at the best possible prices. For example, farmers use WhatsApp to communicate with buyers and sellers, where they receive information on prices, weather forecasts, and other crucial information that helps them make informed decisions.

Print media, such as newspapers, magazines, brochures, and posters, also play a crucial role in agriculture communication in India. Government entities, private companies, and development organizations use print media to disseminate information on market trends, new technologies, and upcoming government policies. The key advantage of print media in India is that it can reach even rural communities who lack access to electronic media. For example, the government of India publishes a monthly bulletin on agriculture in regional languages such as Marathi that reach thousands of farmers across Maharashtra. (Hennik & Bhushan, 2020)

Broadcast media, specifically television and radio, is another communication channel that has proved useful in agriculture-related communication in India. Agricultural TV programs like DD's Kisan and Maharashtra's Krishi Darshan have been highly successful in educating farmers on new technology and best practices in crop management. Similarly, radio remains a popular communication channel in India's rural communities and provides farmers with information on weather updates, market prices, and government schemes. For instance, All India Radio broadcasts daily agricultural schedules that update farmers on all essential agriculture-related information. (Deshpande & Velankar, 2017)

Effective communication is essential in the Indian agricultural context for promoting the industry's growth and sustainability. The different types of communication channels and media used include face-to-face communication, electronic communication, print media, and broadcasting media. By embracing these channels effectively, farmers can access the critical information they need to boost their production and profitability, while stakeholders can collaborate and build trust effectively.

Recent trends in communication channels have emerged in the agricultural context in India, which are worth mentioning. For example, the use of mobile applications for agriculture-related communication is becoming increasingly popular among farmers. Mobile applications like Agri App or CropIn are used to provide farmers with information on weather forecasts, crop management techniques, market prices, crop insurance schemes, and digital farming solutions. These applications have been instrumental in improving the accessibility of agricultural information, especially for small farmers and those living in remote areas. (Fellerman, 2021)

Another recent trend in agricultural communication in India is the use of internet-based platforms. These online platforms are used to connect farmers with potential buyers and sellers across the country. For instance, the Indian government launched an online trading platform called e-NAM (National Agricultural Market), which connects farmers with traders and markets across the country. E-NAM is revolutionizing the way agricultural trade is conducted by eliminating intermediaries and providing farmers with direct access to markets, thereby increasing their profits. (Mudgal et al., 2020)

Recent trends in communication channels and media used in agriculture communication in India have expanded the reach and impact of communication. Mobile applications and internet-based platforms provide farmers with direct access to essential information, while government initiatives like e-NAM have revolutionized the way agricultural trade is conducted. It is crucial to keep up with these trends to promote agricultural growth and sustainability in India. By embracing and exploring these different communication media, Indian agricultural businesses can enhance market opportunities, establish trust among stakeholders, and improve profitability.

1.3 Overview of effective communication strategies and techniques that businesses and cooperative models can use in the agriculture context

Effective communication is vital to the success of cooperative models in the Indian agricultural context. In recent years, cooperatives have emerged as an effective way to promote agricultural growth, particularly in small and fragmented land holdings. The cooperative model is essentially a democratic institution that provides a range of services to its members based on the principle of mutual self-help. Effective communication is critical to the functioning of cooperatives, as it facilitates the exchange of ideas and information between members, management, and other stakeholders. Communication is especially challenging in the Indian agricultural context, where literacy levels are low, and there is a lack of modern technology and infrastructure. This essay provides an overview of effective communication strategies and techniques that cooperative models can use in the Indian agricultural context.

One effective communication strategy that cooperatives can use in the Indian agricultural context is the use of local dialects. In India, there are over 20 official languages, and many dialects spoken across the country. To bridge the language barrier and ensure that all members can understand and participate in the cooperatives' activities, cooperatives can use local dialects that are more easily understood by members. Visual aids such as charts, photographs, and diagrams can also be used to enhance understanding and participation (Bhalerao & Karale, 2019).

Another effective strategy that cooperatives can use is mobile technology. In India, the penetration of mobile devices is very high, and cooperatives can use SMS, voice calls, and mobile apps to provide information and interact with members, stakeholders, and customers. This can also include digital marketing techniques such as online product catalogs, website development, and social media advertising (Patel & Joshi, 2017).

Group discussions are another effective communication technique that cooperatives can use. Group discussions can help members to share information about their experiences, challenges, and opportunities, as well as receive feedback and advice from one another. This can also provide an opportunity to discuss issues related to the cooperative organization, functions, and processes (Gupta & Sharma, 2013).

Training and capacity-building programs can help members develop their skills and knowledge in various agricultural productions, including agricultural finance, management, marketing, and value addition. This can be delivered through face-to-face or online training modules, as well as through video tutorials and manuals. These programs can help members become more productive and efficient and can help the cooperative to gain a reputation for providing valuable services to its members (Singh, 2017).

Cooperatives can also enlist the assistance of government and private sector organizations and non-governmental organizations (NGOs) to offer specialized courses in cooperative education. These courses can help members develop leadership, management, and decision-making skills, as well as cultivate an understanding of the cooperative principles and values. This can help members become more engaged and invested in the cooperative and can help the cooperative to develop strong, capable leaders (Patel & Joshi, 2017).

Finally, internal marketing is an effective communication strategy that cooperatives can use to create and maintain a positive image of the cooperative and its products among its members. This will enhance members' loyalty, encourage product recommendations, and spread positive feedback about the cooperative to potential customers and stakeholders. This can be done through various marketing techniques, including newsletters, brochures, and other promotional materials (Bhalerao & Karale, 2019).

Effective communication is critical to the success of cooperative models in the Indian agricultural context. The use of local dialects, mobile technology, group discussions, training and capacity-building programs, cooperative education, and internal marketing are all effective communication strategies that cooperatives can use to enhance members' participation, efficiency, and productivity and to improve the cooperatives' marketing, risk management, and decision-making processes.

Effective communication plays an important role in the business operations of agriculture in India. It allows companies to build relationships with farmers, better understand their needs and provide them with the necessary support. In this section, we will provide an overview of effective communication strategies and techniques that businesses can use in the agricultural context in India.

One of the most important strategies for effective communication in agriculture businesses is to tailor the message to the audience. This means that companies need to understand the education level, language, culture, and information needs of their farmers. For instance, the use of vernacular languages like Hindi and local dialects can help reach a wider audience in rural areas. Moreover, using pictures, videos, and infographics can increase the impact of the message by making it more relatable and understandable to farmers. (Rasheed, 2019)

Another strategy for effective communication is to build trust with farmers by proactively addressing their concerns. In the agriculture industry, farmers often face challenges related to crop failures, price fluctuations, low-quality inputs, and lack of access to credit. Therefore, companies need to establish a transparent and honest communication system with their farmers to build trust. This can be done by providing farmers with timely and accurate information, explaining the rationale behind business decisions, and offering solutions to their problems. (Erin, 2018)

Communication software and technology also play a key role in modern agricultural communication. For instance, FarmERP is an Indian agricultural enterprise resource planning software that helps businesses manage their various agriculture operations seamlessly. The software can be used to communicate with farmers, manage crop data, predict yields, and monitor agricultural processes in real-time. Moreover, the software allows companies to track the entire supply chain, from production to logistics, including inbound and outbound shipments, to ensure seamless coordination. (Peram, 2020)

Real-time trends and examples of effective communication strategies in agriculture in India include the use of social media platforms like Facebook and Twitter to engage with farmers. For instance, in 2020, the Indian government launched a Twitter handle @KisanCallCenter where farmers can directly call or tweet their concerns related to farming to receive quick and helpful advice. Another example is the use of interactive voice response (IVR) systems to communicate with farmers who live in areas without access to smartphones or the internet. The IVR systems use a computerized voice to interact with farmers, providing them with information on weather forecasts, crop diseases, and market prices. (Venu, 2020)

Effective communication is crucial for businesses to build strong relationships with farmers and succeed in the agricultural sector in India. Tailoring the message to the audience, building trust, and using technology effectively are some of the key strategies for effective communication. The use of software like FarmERP and social media platforms like Twitter, as well as IVR systems, are some examples of effective communication techniques that can be used in the agricultural context in India.

1.4 Developing clear and concise messages for different audiences and stakeholders in agriculture

Developing clear and concise messages is crucial while communicating with diverse stakeholders in agriculture. Communicating agricultural information effectively and persuasively raises farmers' awareness and knowledge, leading to sustainable agricultural practices (Zhang et al., 2021). In India, agriculture is the primary source of livelihood for over 50% of the population and the backbone of the country's economy; hence clear and concise communication in agriculture is essential in driving economic growth and food security (Kumar et al., 2020).

To begin with, it is essential to identify the different stakeholders and their needs. Therefore, before communicating any agricultural message, one must understand their audience's level of knowledge, values, and interests (Wen et al., 2018). In India, agricultural stakeholders include farmers, landowners, agricultural input dealers, farm laborers, government officials, researchers, and different organizations. Each stakeholder has distinct preferences, opinions, and knowledge levels that must be understood and accounted for in the message.

After identifying the target audience, one must develop an appropriate message conveying the intended information. The message must be clear, concise, and straightforward in language, which the stakeholder will understand (Duke et al., 2021). The message must also be tailored to match the stakeholder's interests and needs. For example, a message that appeals to a researcher may not be relevant to a farmer. In India, language diversity is a critical barrier to agricultural communication, demanding that communication is delivered in regional languages to reach a broader audience. Additionally, images, videos, and demonstration of best practices are effective ways to communicate in agriculture apart from verbal communication.

The message delivered must be relevant to the stakeholder, easy to understand, and actionable. Information should be emphasized clearly to provide an idea of what can be adopted, applied, or changed based on accurate data and factual statements. Messages should be accompanied by tangible solutions and alternatives that are practical. For instance, in India, effective communication to farmers would entail delivering comprehensive information about the latest varieties of crops with low water requirements or providing the most appropriate practices that boost productivity and ensure sustainability, thereby enhancing participation in adaptation strategies (Kumar et al., 2020).

Finally, actively listening to feedback from stakeholders is essential to improve communication effectiveness. The feedback allows you to evaluate whether the message delivered was relevant, accurate, and actionable. Feedback from the farmers, agricultural organizations, and other stakeholders is essential as it provides an opportunity to tailor communication based on stakeholder feedback and needs (Wen et al., 2018). In India, feedback can be obtained through several ways, including focus group discussions, community meetings, surveys, or direct field interaction.

Communication in agriculture is critical in promoting sustainable farming practices, leading to economic growth and food security in India. Communicating effectively requires identifying the diverse audience's interests, and developing clear, concise, and tailored messages that align with stakeholder objectives. Rationalizing the message and tailoring it to the stakeholder's values, interests, and language preference is essential in ensuring the stakeholders' needs are met. Monitoring feedback and evaluating successes is a continuous process for communicating through different audience messages, thereby enhancing effectiveness, sustainability, and enhancing participation in agricultural growth.

1.5 Overview of different types of reports and their purposes, and guidelines to prepare them

Reports are essential documents used to communicate findings, analyses, and recommendations derived from research, fieldwork, or other forms of data collection. They play a vital role in the agricultural sector, particularly in India, where most of the population relies on agriculture, and the sector contributes significantly to the economy (Kumar et al., 2020). Understanding different types of reports and their purposes is crucial for any individual involved in agriculture. This chapter provides an overview of different types of reports, their purposes, and how to prepare them in an agricultural context in India.

The first type of report is the research report. A research report documents the research process, findings, and recommendations from a study. Research reports in agriculture can range from research on soil fertility, crop production, yield, or market trends (Deb et al., 2019). The primary purpose of a research report is to communicate the findings and recommendations in a clear and concise manner. The report should include a detailed description of the study's methodology, data analysis, and findings with supporting graphs and charts. In India, research reports are essential for driving evidence-based policies, guiding decision-making, and building a knowledge base for the sector (Kumar et al., 2020).

A project progress report is another significant type of report in agriculture. It documents the progress of a particular project and informs stakeholders of the ongoing activities. The report should include updates on project milestones, timelines, budget, and any challenges, with recommendations for mitigation. Timely submission of project progress reports is essential to keep stakeholders informed and ensure accountability by the project team. In India, project progress reports are commonly prepared by Non-Governmental Organizations (NGOs) documenting their developmental and outreach projects in agriculture.

The third type of report is the evaluation report. An evaluation report documents the assessment of a program or project performance. Evaluation reports should provide an objective assessment of the project or program's impact, effectiveness, and sustainability (FAO, 2017). The report should include an analysis of the strengths, weaknesses, opportunities, and threats (SWOT), with detailed recommendations for improvement. In India, evaluation reports play a crucial role in ensuring accountability and transparency in agriculture, particularly in public-funded projects.

Periodic reports are another essential type of report in agriculture. Periodic reports are prepared at scheduled intervals, such as monthly, bi-annually, or annually, and document the ongoing activities, challenges, achievements, plans, and recommendations of an organization or project. Periodic reports help stakeholders track progress and measure outcomes over time, allowing timely decision-making and intervention where necessary. For example, in India, periodic reports in the agriculture sector are prepared by state agriculture departments as part of their assessment and projection of agricultural growth over successive years.

The next type of report is the executive summary, which is a brief overview of a longer report. The purpose of an executive summary is to provide the reader with a summary of the main points of the report, without having to read the entire document. This type of report is useful for busy stakeholders who need to quickly understand the key findings of the report. (EPA, 2018)

Then there is technical report, which provides a detailed analysis of a particular issue, such as soil fertility, crop yields, or pest control measures. Technical reports are typically more detailed than executive summaries and may include graphs, charts, and other data visualizations. The purpose of a technical report is to provide stakeholders with a deeper understanding of specific issues related to agriculture. (Joshi, 2018)

Reports play a critical role in the agricultural sector in India. Different types of reports serve distinct purposes and are essential for driving evidence-based policies, decision-making, and building knowledge bases. Preparing reports requires a clear understanding of the intended purpose, target audience, and the message to be conveyed. Therefore, one must ensure the report is clear, concise, and structured, including visual components such as tables and graphs to enhance readability for the target audience.

To prepare a report in the Indian agricultural context, it is important to follow certain guidelines. Firstly, the report should be written in a clear and concise manner, avoiding technical jargon or complex terminology wherever possible. Secondly, the report should be structured into clear sections, with headings and subheadings to guide the reader. Thirdly, the report should include relevant data, statistics, and facts to support the findings of the report. (Agrilinks, 2020)

Real-time examples of reports in Indian agriculture include the State of Indian Agriculture Report published by the Ministry of Agriculture and Farmers' Welfare. The report provides an overview of the state of agriculture in India, including crop production, area under cultivation, and livestock rearing. Another example is the Annual Report of the Indian Council of Agricultural Research, which provides an overview of the research activities carried out by the council in different fields of agriculture. (Govt. of India, 2020)

Software like FarmERP can also be used to prepare and manage reports in the agricultural context in India. The software allows businesses to manage all aspects of their agricultural operations, from production to supply chain, logistics, and financial management. The software also provides real-time analytics and reporting, allowing businesses to monitor their performance and make informed decisions based on the data. (Peram, 2020)

Reports play an important role in the agricultural context in India, communicating information to different stakeholders. Different types of reports have different purposes and require specific guidelines for preparation.

1.6 Best practices and case studies of businesses and cooperative models that have successfully used effective communication strategies and techniques in an agricultural context

Effective communication strategies and techniques are vital in agriculture to create awareness among farmers about new technologies and farming practices to increase production and profitability. In India, several businesses have successfully implemented communication strategies to promote their products and services. This part highlights some of the best practices and case studies of businesses that have successfully used effective communication strategies in the agricultural context in India.

One of the best practices observed is the use of digital platforms such as social media, mobile applications, and websites to disseminate information to farmers. For example, CropIn is an agricultural technology company that provides farm management solutions to farmers. They have developed a mobile application that enables farmers to manage their farms efficiently and provides real-time data on weather patterns, crop growth, and market prices. Through the application, farmers can also interact with CropIn's agronomists and crop experts for advice and support.

Another best practice is the use of village-level programs to engage with farmers and provide them with training and education on new farming practices. Mahindra & Mahindra, a leading tractor manufacturer in India, has implemented such a program called Krishi Samridhi, which aims to educate farmers on efficient and sustainable farming practices. The program includes training sessions, demonstrations, and interactions with experts in the field. As a result, over 90% of the participating farmers have reported an increase in yield and profitability.

Additionally, businesses have successfully used influencer marketing to promote their products and services. For example, Cargill, a global food and agricultural company, launched a campaign called "Soulfull Jeevika" in collaboration with popular YouTubers in India. The campaign aimed to promote the Soulfull brand of millet-based snacks and promote the benefits of millets for health and sustainability. As a result of the campaign, there was a significant increase in demand for millets, and Soulfull products gained popularity among consumers.

One more of the best practices of effective communication in agriculture is building relationships with stakeholders. A case in point is the partnership between Absolute Organics and the Maati cooperative in Meghalaya. (IndiaAgroNet) The partnership is aimed at promoting sustainable agriculture practices, and the two entities have created a platform for farmers to sell their organic produce directly to consumers. Through effective communication, Absolute Organics has built a strong relationship with the farmers, which has led to increased productivity and profitability for both parties.

Another best practice of effective communication in agriculture is educating stakeholders. In India, many small-scale farmers lack access to information on modern agricultural practices. However, companies like ITC Limited have taken the initiative to educate farmers through its e-Choupal initiative. (The Better India) The e-Choupal initiative provides farmers with access to information on weather patterns, soil management, and crop cultivation techniques. This has improved the productivity of the farmers and has helped to create a sustainable agricultural ecosystem.

Effective communication can also be used to improve supply chain management in agriculture. A case in point is the partnership between the Cambodian Agriculture Cooperative Corporation (CACC) and the German retail giant, Metro AG. (Business Wire) Through effective communication, CACC has been able to streamline its supply chain and improve its distribution channels. The partnership has helped CACC to export large quantities of bananas to Metro AG, thereby boosting its profitability.

Furthermore, building a strong brand through effective communication is important in agriculture. A case in point is the brand-building efforts of Mother Dairy in India. (India Tribune) Mother Dairy has built a powerful brand through its communication efforts, which has helped to boost sales and created a loyal customer base. The company has focused on communicating its values to its customers, including its commitment to quality and sustainability. Effective communication is critical for the success of agriculture businesses in India. Building relationships with stakeholders, educating farmers, improving supply chain management, and building a strong brand are some of the best practices for effective communication in agriculture. Through effective communication, businesses can improve productivity, and profitability, and create a sustainable agricultural ecosystem.

Cooperative models that use effective communication strategies and techniques play a crucial role in facilitating the exchange of ideas and information between members and other stakeholders. The use of modern information and communication technologies, local languages, and the involvement of government and private sector organizations in training and capacity building are some of the key strategies that have been adopted by cooperative models to enhance communication. This essay provides an overview of best practices and case studies of cooperative models that have successfully used effective communication strategies and techniques in agriculture.

One of the best practices that cooperative models use is the use of mobile technologies for communication, especially in regions where there is limited access to the internet. The West Bengal Livelihoods Development Corporation (WBLDC) has successfully used mobile technologies to provide timely information to farmers on weather, market prices, and pest and disease management. The use of automated voice calls and SMSs in the local language helps to reach more farmers, including women and those who are illiterate. The impact of this intervention has been significant, as farmers have been able to improve their yields and incomes (Kundu et al., 2018).

Another best practice is the use of group discussions as a means of enhancing communication and building the capacity of members. The Dairy Development Cooperative Society in Rajasthan, India, uses group discussions to share information on various aspects of dairy farming, including feeding and management practices, and marketing strategies. These discussions have also helped to build a sense of community among the members, resulting in increased cooperation and solidarity (Gupta & Sharma, 2013).

Cooperatives that involve members in the decision-making process also have better communication channels. The Sangha Mitra Agro Producers Company (SAPCO), a farmer-owned cooperative in Karnataka, India, engages members in the governance and management of the cooperative. Members sit on committees that oversee various aspects of the cooperative's operations, including finance, marketing, and quality assurance. This approach has led to greater ownership of the cooperative and high levels of member participation, leading to better communication and improved performance (Nelson & Shankar, 2017).

The use of local languages and visual aids is another best practice that cooperatives use. The Kisan Vikas Gramin Sanstha (KVGMS), a farmer-owned cooperative in Uttar Pradesh, India, uses local languages and visual aids to communicate with their members. The cooperative has developed posters and videos in the local language to educate farmers on best farming practices and the risks associated with pesticide use. The cooperative targets women, a key segment of their membership, through women's groups that have been formed to provide training on kitchen gardening and livestock care (Kumar et al., 2020).

Effective communication strategies and techniques play a significant role in the success of cooperative models in agriculture. Best practices such as mobile technologies, group discussions, involving members in the decision-making process, and the use of local languages and visual aids have been successfully adopted by cooperative models. These strategies improve communication channels between members and other stakeholders leading to improved decision making and better agricultural practices. Cooperative models such as the West Bengal Livelihoods Development Corporation, Dairy Development Cooperative Society, Sangha Mitra Agro Producers Company, and Kisan Vikas Gramin Sanstha provide successful case studies of the use of effective communication strategies.

Appendix

General guidelines for business report

1. ***Purpose and Scope:*** Clearly state the purpose and scope of the business report. Explain the background, context, and rationale for the report.
2. ***Methodology:*** Describe the methods used for collecting data, analyzing information, and presenting findings. Use clear and concise language and include relevant data, tables, charts, and graphs.
3. ***Results:*** Summarize the key findings of the report. Present the data, trends, and patterns that support the conclusions. Be objective, precise, and factual in your presentation.
4. ***Analysis:*** Analyze the implications of the findings for the agricultural industry, its stakeholders, and the broader community. Discuss the strengths, weaknesses, opportunities, and challenges of the industry and provide recommendations for improvement.
5. ***Conclusion:*** Summarize the main points of the report and highlight its implications for agriculture students. Provide a clear and concise conclusion that ties together all the main themes and arguments of the report.
6. ***References:*** Cite all the sources used in the report in a systematic and accurate way. Use appropriate referencing styles, such as APA, MLA, or Chicago, and double-check all the citations and references for accuracy and completeness.
7. ***Appendix:*** Include all the supporting material, such as data sheets, survey questionnaires, interview transcripts, and other relevant documents, in the

appendix. Use clear and consistent labels for each item in the appendix to facilitate easy reference.

Chapter Section Summaries

1.1: Definition of business communication and its role in agriculture

This part focused on the essential nature of communication in the agriculture industry. It covered the definition of business communication and its significance in promoting productivity, profitability, and sustainability in agriculture. The objectives of this part of the chapter were to define business communication, highlight its importance in agriculture, and evaluate the impact of effective communication in agriculture.

1.2: Overview of different types of communication channels and media used in business communication

This part provided an in-depth analysis of various communication channels and media utilised in business communication. It highlighted the significance of selecting the right medium for conveying your message effectively. The objectives of this chapter were to classify the various communication channels and media, reflect on the role of different mediums, and evaluate the relevance of different mediums in agricultural communication.

1.3: Overview of effective communication strategies and techniques that businesses and co-operative models can use in agricultural context

This part covered strategies and techniques that businesses and cooperative models use in agricultural communication. It offered practical tips and best practices for designing effective communication plans that produce successful outcomes for the business. The objectives of this chapter were to identify common barriers to effective communication in agriculture, explain the principles of effective communication strategies, and evaluate the effectiveness of different communication techniques in agriculture.

1.4: Developing clear and concise messages for different audiences and stakeholders

This chapter covered how to develop clear and concise messages that reach and engage different stakeholders. It offered insights into techniques for developing messages that communicate effectively with various audiences, including suppliers, customers, shareholders, and employees. The objectives of this chapter were to define clear and concise messaging, create messages that communicate effectively with different stakeholders, and identify best practices for the development of clear and concise messages in agricultural communication.

1.5: Overview of different types of reports and their purposes, and how to prepare them

This part focused on different types of reports used in agricultural communication, including operational, analytical, and persuasive. It outlined the various purposes for which each report type is suited and provides guidelines on how to produce professional-quality reports that meet the business's desired outcomes. The objectives of this chapter were to describe the purpose of different report types, how to prepare and format reports for effective communication, and the importance of different reports in agriculture.

1.6: Best Practices and case studies of Businesses and cooperative models that have successfully used effective communication Strategies and Techniques in Agriculture

This part detailed case studies of successful agricultural businesses that have effectively employed different communication strategies and techniques. The examples provided insights into how to design effective communication strategies that promote productivity, profitability, and sustainability. The objectives of this chapter were to analyze best practices used by successful agricultural businesses, evaluate case studies of successful agricultural businesses, and develop strategies and techniques for effective communication in agriculture based on best practices and case studies.

Discussion Questions

1-1 How does effective business communication impact the productivity of the agriculture industry?

1-2 What are the differences between written and verbal communication, and how might they impact agriculture businesses?

1-3 How can a communication strategy be created or optimized for best-achieving farm or agricultural business goals?

1-4 Using an example of a potential stakeholder, write a message that effectively communicates important details about a new agricultural product.

1-5 How might an evaluation report differ in format from an investigative report in conveying the results of a study on soil contamination?

1-6 Using a case study of a successful agricultural business and co-operative models, identify the most effective communication strategies and explain why those strategies were successful.

Application Cases

Case Study 1: Gujarat Cooperative Milk Marketing Federation (GCMMF)

Gujarat Cooperative Milk Marketing Federation (GCMMF), also known as Amul, is the largest dairy cooperative in India. It was founded in 1946 by Tribhuvandas Patel and has grown to include over 3.6 million milk-producing members from over 18,500 villages across Gujarat. GCMMF is responsible for the marketing and sale of various dairy products, including milk, butter, cheese, and ice cream. It operates through a network of 18 member unions that collect milk from farmers and process it into various products at various facilities.

GCMMF is known for its successful branding and marketing initiatives, including the famous Amul Girl advertising campaign. The cooperative has also leveraged social media platforms to engage with its customers and promote its products. In recent years, the cooperative has faced competition from international dairy companies that are increasingly targeting the Indian market. Despite these challenges, GCMMF has continued to grow and expand its operations both within India and internationally.

GCMMF, also known as Amul, is a well-established dairy cooperative in India. Despite its success, the organization is facing some significant challenges that threaten its growth and sustainability. The Board of Directors of GCMMF has hired you as a communications consultant to develop a strategic plan that addresses these challenges and ensures the long-term viability of the cooperative. The challenges facing the cooperative include:

1. Stiff competition from international dairy companies that are aggressively marketing their products in the Indian market.
2. Discontent among some of the member farmers who feel that they are not being fairly compensated for their milk.
3. Limited understanding among consumers about the benefits of consuming dairy products.
4. Changing consumer preferences towards non-dairy milk substitutes.
5. The need to explore new markets beyond India to sustain growth.

Case study questions

1. What communication strategies can GCMMF employ to mitigate the impact of stiff competition from foreign dairy companies?
2. How can GCMMF effectively communicate with member farmers to address their concerns?

3. What kind of communication initiatives can GCMMF use to raise consumers' awareness about the benefits of consuming dairy products?
4. How can GCMMF address the changing consumer preferences towards non-dairy milk substitutes?
5. What communication strategies can GCMMF use to expand into new markets?

Case Study 2: Sangha Mitra Agro Producers Company (SAPCO)

The Sangha Mitra Agro Producers Company (SAPCO) is a social enterprise in the agriculture industry that aims to uplift farmers in rural areas by providing them with fair prices for their produce and improving their production practices. For the past few years, SAPCO has been experiencing communication challenges that have hindered their operations and growth.

SAPCO recently secured a large contract with a national food retailer to supply them with organic vegetables and fruits. This was a significant milestone for the company, and they were excited to fulfill the contract. However, after a few weeks of delivery, the retailer started receiving complaints from its customers that the produce was of low quality and not meeting their expectations. SAPCO received this feedback from the retailer and was surprised that their produce was being rejected despite going through their stringent quality control procedures. They reached out to the farmers and found out that they were using outdated production techniques and had poor access to information and resources.

SAPCO realized that there was a significant communication gap between the farmers and the company, and they needed to find a way to bridge it. They also recognized that they needed to improve their communication processes with the food retailer to ensure that they met their quality standards and maintained the contract.

Challenges

SAPCO faced several communication challenges in this scenario:

1. Farmer communication: Many of the farmers that SAPCO worked with did not have access to modern communication channels and were using outdated farming techniques. This made it difficult for SAPCO to keep them informed about the latest production practices and maintain quality standards.
2. Internal communication: There was a lack of internal communication within SAPCO, resulting in miscommunication, poor coordination, and delays in decision-making.

3. Retailer communication: SAPCO did not have a clear understanding of the retailer's communication channels and preferred format for receiving communication. This resulted in miscommunication and the rejection of SAPCO's produce.

Communication Strategies and Techniques

To overcome these communication challenges and improve SAPCO's operations, several communication strategies and techniques could be utilized:

1. Enhancing Farmer Communication: SAPCO could work on educating farmers on the latest production techniques and provide them with access to modern communication channels such as mobile phones, radio, and the internet. This would enable them to stay informed about market prices, new farming practices, and weather conditions, which would ultimately help improve their produce quality.
2. Improving Internal Communication: SAPCO could implement an internal communication system that would enable employees to share information, updates, and feedback effectively. This could be in the form of a centralized platform such as a company intranet, a communication app, or regular team meetings.
3. Effective Retailer Communication: SAPCO could obtain a clear understanding of the retailer's communication channels and preferred format of communication. They could then tailor their communication to meet those preferences and create reports that provide detailed information about the produce quality, production processes, and delivery schedules.

Channels and Types of Communication

To ensure effective communication, SAPCO could use various channels and types of communication, such as:

1. Mobile phones: SAPCO could use SMS, voice calls, or instant messaging to communicate with farmers and provide them with regular updates about market prices, produce quality, and new farming practices.
2. Company intranet: SAPCO could use a centralized platform where employees could share updates, feedback, and information. The platform could also have features such as forums, chat rooms, and document sharing.
3. Reports: SAPCO could create detailed reports for the retailer that provide information about the produce quality, production processes, and delivery schedules. These reports could be in a format that is preferred by the retailer, such as Excel spreadsheets or PDFs.

In summary, effective communication is critical for the success of any organization. SAPCO faced numerous communication challenges that hindered their growth and affected the quality of their produce. By implementing communication strategies and techniques such as enhancing farmer communication, improving internal communication, and effective retailer communication and utilizing various communication channels and types, SAPCO can address these challenges and elevate their operations and production.

Case study questions

1. What were the communication challenges faced by SAPCO in the scenario provided?
2. How did SAPCO address the communication challenges faced by them in the scenario provided?
3. Can you suggest any other communication strategies and techniques that SAPCO could have utilized to overcome its communication challenges?
4. What impact did the communication challenges faced by SAPCO have on their operations and growth?
5. How would you create a comprehensive communication plan for SAPCO that addresses their communication challenges and ensures effective communication within the organization and with their stakeholders such as farmers and retailers?

References

Agrilinks. (2020). Tips for effective reporting. https://www.agrilinks.org/blog/tips-effective-reporting

Bhalerao, P., & Karale, A. (2019). Communication Strategies of Agricultural Cooperatives in India: A Case Study of Maharashtra. Indian Journal of Agricultural Marketing, 33(2), 58-65.

Business Wire- https://www.businesswireindia.com/

Cargill. (n.d.). Soulfull Jeevika. Retrieved from https://www.cargill.com/2018/soulfull-jeevika

CropIn. (n.d.). Our Product. Retrieved from https://www.cropin.com/overview/

Deb, K., Meltzer, R. M., & Sundaresan, S. (2019). The impact of native mobile applications on the adoption of agricultural information systems: An empirical study from India. Journal of Agribusiness in Developing and Emerging Economies, 9(4), 462-480.

Deshpande, G., & Velankar, H. (2017). Role of mass media in agriculture Extension: A Review Paper. Retrieved from http://nopr.niscair.res.in/bitstream/123456789/43266/1/JIPR%2022(1)%2046-50.pdf

Duke, A. J., III, Daniel, G. C., & Wohlgemuth, K. Y. (2021). Communication strategies for agricultural producers and urban publics in the western US: A media analysis. Journal of Extension, 59(3), n3.

EPA. (2018). What is an executive summary?https://www.epa.gov/grants/what-executive-summary

Erin, K. (2018). Building trust with farmers: Communication strategies for agribusiness success. Ohio Ag Net. https://www.ocj.com/2018/07/building-trust-with-farmers-communication-strategies-for-agribusiness-success/

FAO (2017). Preparing Evaluation Reports: A Concise Guide for UNDP Staff. United Nations Development Programme. Retrieved from https://www.undp.org/content/dam/undp/library/corporate/Operations/Evaluation/evaluations/eguidePreparingEvaluationReports.pdf

FAO. (2016). Guidelines for preparing progress reports. http://www.fao.org/3/a-i6346e.pdf

Fellerman, M. (2021). Smart Farming in India: The Role of Agricultural Mobile Apps. Agroop. https://agroop.net/smart-farming-india-agricultural-mobile-apps/

Govt. of India. (2020). Reports. https://www.india.gov.in/topics/agriculture/reports/

Gupta, R. K., & Sharma, S. (2013). Effective communication strategies for agricultural development: A case study of cooperative societies in Rajasthan, India. African Journal of Agricultural Research, 8(6), 551-557.

Gupta, R. K., & Sharma, S. (2013). Effective communication strategies for agricultural development: A case study of cooperative societies in Rajasthan, India. African Journal of Agricultural Research, 8(6), 551-557.

Hennink, M., & Bhushan, R. (2020). What Is The Future For Global Agriculture: How India Can Lead Productivity Gains. Retrieved from https://www.forbes.com/sites/markhennick/2020/02/21/what-is-the-future-for-global-agriculture-how-india-can-lead-productivity-gains/?sh=1ef0adf0cfd6

https://www.cargill.co.in/

https://www.cropin.com/

IndiaAgroNet - https://indiaagronet.com/indiaagronet/agronet_home/agrinethome.htm

India Tribune - https://www.indiatribune.com/mother-dairy-focuses-on-building-a-brand/

Joshi, R. (2018). Technical report writing for agriculture students. Journal of Agricultural Science and Technology, 1(2), 50-59.

Kumar, P., Nainawat, R., & Anwar, S. (2020). Advancements in Agriculture Extension System in India: A Review. International Journal of Agriculture Extension, 8(1), 213-221

Kumar, R., Singh, R., & Kumar, V. (2020). Women Empowerment Through Farmer Producer Organization in India: A Case Study of Kisan Vikas Gramin Sanstha. International Journal of Agricultural Sciences, 12(40), 19-21.

Kundu, S., Pal, A., Majumder, U., Maiti, S., & Chatterjee, D. (2018). A Study on the Impact of Mobile Based Agricultural Information Services on Socio-Economic Empowerment of Farmers: An Evidence from West Bengal, India. Indian Journal of Agricultural Economics, 73(1), 30-41.

Landes, M. K. (2014). Agricultural cooperatives in India: Role, performance and impact. International Journal of Agricultural Management, 3(3), 129-139.

Mahindra & Mahindra. (n.d.). Mahindra Krishi Samridhi. Retrieved from https://www.mahindra.com/our-businesses/Farm-Equipment/mahindra-krishi-samridhi

Maulik, S. R., & Debnath, T. (2013). Impact of Communication on Behaviour of Farmers. Agricultural Economics Research Review, 26(2), 261-270.

Mudgal, S., Singh, S., & Chauhan, V. K. (2020). e-NAM: The National Agricultural Market of India. International Journal of Engineering and Advanced Technology, 9(1), 238-244.

Nelson, S., & Shankar, B. (2017). An investigation of the effectiveness of farmer producer organizations in improving smallholder farmers' income: a case study of Sangha Mitra Agro Producers Company. Agricultural and Food Economics, 5(1), 1-19.

Patel, S. K., & Joshi, P. K. (2017). Role of ICTs in enhancing effectiveness of agricultural cooperatives in India. Agricultural Economics Research Review, 30(2), 283-291.

Peram, S. (2020). The role of an integrated Agri ERP software in improving agriculture in India. FarmERP. https://www.farmerp.com/the-role-of-an-integrated-agri-erp-software-in-improving-agriculture-in-india

Rasheed, A. (2019). Communication strategies for improving agricultural extension services in India. Journal of Agricultural Extension and Rural Development, 11(4), 75-78.

Singh, J. P. (2017). Role of Cooperatives in Agricultural Development in India: A Study on Dairy Cooperatives. Journal of Entrepreneurship, Management and Innovation, 13(3), 19-43

The Better India - https://www.thebetterindia.com/

Venu, M. (2020). Interactive Voice Response (IVR) system: A tool for effective dissemination of agricultural information. Indian Streams Research Journal, 10(10), 1-4.

Wen, L., Zhong, R., Zhou, Y., Liu, X., Xie, R., & Gao, L. (2018). Communicating food safety and technological risk in an emerging online environment: Perceptions of key stakeholders in the Chinese agrifood supply chain. Food control, 89, 186-195.

Zhang, J., Ju, X., Li, P., and Duan, Y. (2021). The Influence of Agricultural Information on Farmers' Willingness to Adopt Technologies: Evidence from Northeast China. Journal of Agriculture, Food Systems, and Community Development, 10(1), 15-30.

2

Impact of COVID-19 on Agribusiness Communications

Introduction

The COVID-19 pandemic has significantly impacted agribusiness communications, creating unprecedented challenges and opportunities for the sector. With restrictions on transportation, shortage of labor, and changes in consumer behavior, agribusinesses have had to adapt their communication strategies to remain operational and retain consumer trust. The objective of this chapter is to analyze the impact of the COVID-19 pandemic on agribusiness communication and suggest effective communication strategies to overcome the challenges posed by this and similar crisis which might arise in the future.

Learning Objectives

2-1. Understand the impact of the COVID-19 pandemic on the agribusiness value chain.

The COVID-19 pandemic has disrupted every aspect of the agribusiness value chain, affecting production, supply, and demand. The part will discuss the implications of this disruption for agribusiness communication and share best practices for effective stakeholder communication.

2-2. Analyze the role of social media during the COVID-19 pandemic in agribusiness communication.

The use of social media by agribusinesses has increased exponentially during the pandemic. The part will explore the role of social media in building brand awareness, engaging with consumers, and sharing critical information about the agribusiness value chain.

2-3. Evaluate the effectiveness of crisis communication strategies adopted by agribusinesses during the pandemic.

The COVID-19 pandemic has tested the crisis communication capabilities of agribusinesses. The part will evaluate the effectiveness of crisis communication strategies used by agribusinesses in addressing the challenges posed by this crisis.

2.4. Understand the role of government policies on agribusiness communication during the pandemic.

Government policies have played a critical role in shaping the agribusiness communication strategies during the COVID-19 pandemic. The part will analyze the impact of government policies on agribusiness communication and suggest effective ways for agribusinesses to engage with policymakers.

2.5. Evaluate the use of e-commerce and digitalization in agribusiness communication during the pandemic.

The pandemic has accelerated the adoption of e-commerce and digitalization in agribusiness communication. The part will evaluate the effectiveness of digital communication channels and their impact on consumer behavior and agribusiness operations during the pandemic.

2.6. Analyze case studies on agribusiness communication during the pandemic.

The part will present case studies on a successful agribusiness communication strategy adopted by a leading agribusiness company during the COVID-19 pandemic. The case studies will provide insights into the challenges faced by the company, the solutions adopted, and the impact of these solutions on its stakeholders.

The COVID-19 pandemic has reshaped the way agribusinesses communicate with their stakeholders. Agribusinesses need to adopt innovative communication strategies to address the challenges posed by this crisis effectively. The part has outlined six learning objectives that will provide a comprehensive understanding of the impact of the COVID-19 pandemic on agribusiness communication. The last objective will provide a practical example of how a leading agribusiness company overcame the challenges posed by the pandemic through effective communication strategies. The part offers insights into the best practices for agribusiness communication during the crisis and beyond.

2.1 Impact of COVID-19 on the Agribusiness Value Chain: Implications for Communication Strategies

The COVID-19 pandemic has disrupted the agribusiness value chain, causing significant challenges for farmers, processors, and distributors (Swinnen et al., 2020). Restrictions on movement and closure of markets have resulted in the loss of produce and reduced income for farmers across the globe. Similarly, processors and distributors have struggled to keep their businesses functioning due to a shortage of labor and changes in consumer behavior (Amuedo-Dorantes & Sarzosa, 2020). The crisis has highlighted the need for effective communication strategies to maintain customer trust, manage stakeholder expectations, and address the challenges posed by the pandemic.

Agribusinesses are dynamic organizations that need to navigate complex relationships with a diverse range of stakeholders. The COVID-19 pandemic has magnified the importance of clear and effective communication strategies in maintaining these relationships. Effective communication strategies can help agribusinesses address the uncertainties associated with the pandemic and maintain trust with their stakeholders. A recent study has identified five communication strategies that can be helpful for agribusinesses in the context of the pandemic: timely and transparent communication, personalization, empathy, two-way communication, and stakeholder engagement (Wang et al., 2020).

Timely and transparent communication is critical during the COVID-19 pandemic since the situation is rapidly evolving. Stakeholders need to be informed about any changes that may affect their interests. Personalization of communication strategies helps build trust between the agribusinesses and stakeholders. Communicating with empathy and sensitivity towards the customer's needs can help agribusinesses address the emotional stress and uncertainties faced by stakeholders. Two-way communication can help agribusinesses adapt their communication strategies based on feedback from stakeholders. Stakeholder engagement through collaboration on decision-making can help agribusinesses build trust and confidence with their stakeholders (Wang et al., 2020).

Several agribusinesses have embraced these communication strategies and have been able to maintain customer trust during the pandemic. For example, Dole Foods used social media to keep their customers informed about their operation during the pandemic and the measures they were taking to ensure their safety (The Packer, 2020). Similarly, Tyson Foods used their website and social media to communicate with their stakeholders and inform them about the measures they were taking to provide safe and healthy products (Tyson Foods, 2020). The communication of such strategies has demonstrated a strong commitment to the customers' health and safety and has helped these companies maintain the stakeholders' confidence in their brands.

The COVID-19 pandemic has presented unprecedented challenges to the agribusiness value chain. Effective communication strategies are essential to maintain stakeholder trust, address the challenges posed by the pandemic, and remain operational. Clear communication that is transparent, personalized, empathetic, and engages stakeholders can help agribusinesses navigate the crisis successfully. Agribusinesses that embrace effective communication strategies can emerge even stronger from the pandemic.

2.2 Leveraging Social Media for Effective Agribusiness Communication during the Pandemic

The COVID-19 pandemic has disrupted the agribusiness value chain, causing significant challenges for farmers, processors, and distributors (Swinnen et al., 2020). Restrictions on movement and closure of markets have resulted in the loss of produce and reduced income for farmers across the globe. Similarly, processors and distributors have struggled to keep their businesses functioning due to a shortage of labor and changes in consumer behavior (Amuedo-Dorantes & Sarzosa, 2020). The crisis has highlighted the need for effective communication strategies to maintain customer trust, manage stakeholder expectations, and address the challenges posed by the pandemic.

Agribusinesses are dynamic organizations that need to navigate complex relationships with a diverse range of stakeholders. The COVID-19 pandemic has magnified the importance of clear and effective communication strategies in maintaining these relationships. Effective communication strategies can help agribusinesses address the uncertainties associated with the pandemic and maintain trust with their stakeholders. A recent study has identified five communication strategies that can be helpful for agribusinesses in the context of the pandemic: timely and transparent communication, personalization, empathy, two-way communication, and stakeholder engagement (Wang et al., 2020).

Timely and transparent communication is critical during the COVID-19 pandemic since the situation is rapidly evolving. Stakeholders need to be informed about any changes that may affect their interests. Personalization of communication strategies helps build trust between the agribusinesses and stakeholders. Communicating with empathy and sensitivity towards the customer's needs can help agribusinesses address the emotional stress and uncertainties faced by stakeholders. Two-way communication can help agribusinesses adapt their communication strategies based on feedback from stakeholders. Stakeholder engagement through collaboration on decision-making can help agribusinesses build trust and confidence with their stakeholders (Wang et al., 2020).

Several agribusinesses have embraced these communication strategies and have been able to maintain customer trust during the pandemic. For example, Dole Foods used social media to keep their customers informed about their operation during the pandemic and the measures they were taking to ensure their safety (The Packer, 2020). Similarly, Tyson Foods used their website and social media to communicate with their stakeholders and inform them about the measures they were taking to provide safe and healthy products

(Tyson Foods, 2020). The communication of such strategies has demonstrated a strong commitment to the customers' health and safety and has helped these companies maintain the stakeholders' confidence in their brands.

The COVID-19 pandemic has hit the Indian agribusiness sector hard, with disruptions in the supply chain and logistics. In this context, leveraging social media platforms for effective communication has become increasingly important. In this section, we will explore how Indian agribusinesses can use social media to communicate with their stakeholders during the pandemic, along with examples of companies that have successfully implemented these strategies.

Indian agribusinesses can use social media platforms such as Facebook, Twitter, Instagram, and WhatsApp to communicate with their stakeholders during the pandemic. Agribusinesses can use these platforms to share updates on operational changes, supply chain disruptions, and new products or services. Additionally, social media can help agribusinesses to address the concerns and queries of their customers and build trust and loyalty among them (Chowdhury et al., 2020).

Several Indian agribusinesses have successfully implemented social media communication strategies during the pandemic. For example, AgriBazaar, an agricultural e-commerce company, used WhatsApp to connect with farmers and buyers and helped them overcome logistical challenges caused by the pandemic. AgriBazaar launched a "Farm to Fork" campaign to encourage farmers to sell their produce directly to consumers through the platform. AgriBazaar also used YouTube and Facebook to showcase success stories of farmers who used the platform and to educate farmers on the benefits of using digital platforms to sell their produce (AgriBazaar, 2020).

Similarly, Ninjacart, a B2B agri-tech start-up, used social media platforms to communicate with customers and stakeholders during the pandemic. Ninjacart used WhatsApp to communicate with customers about new products, offers, and discounts. Ninjacart also used social media to educate farmers on how to adopt best practices for increasing crop yield and improving quality. In addition, Ninjacart launched a "Ninja Fund" campaign to provide financial assistance to farmers affected by the pandemic (Ninjacart, 2020).

Social media platforms can be a valuable communication tool for Indian agribusinesses during the pandemic. Agribusinesses can use social media platforms to communicate with their stakeholders quickly, effectively, and in a cost-effective manner. Implementing these strategies can help Indian agribusinesses navigate the challenges posed by the COVID-19 pandemic successfully.

The COVID-19 pandemic has presented unprecedented challenges to the agribusiness value chain. Effective communication strategies are essential to maintain stakeholder trust, address the challenges posed by the pandemic, and remain operational. Clear communication that is transparent, personalized, empathetic, and engages stakeholders can help agribusinesses navigate the crisis successfully. Agribusinesses that embrace effective communication strategies can emerge even stronger from the pandemic.

In India, agribusiness companies such as AgriBazaar and Ninjacart have successfully leveraged social media to communicate with their stakeholders during the pandemic. AgriBazaar used WhatsApp, YouTube, and Facebook to connect with farmers and buyers and educate them on the benefits of using the platform for selling and buying produce directly. Ninjacart used WhatsApp and social media platforms to communicate with customers, provide financial assistance to farmers, and educate farmers on best practices for increasing crop yield and quality.

The success of these companies demonstrates the potential of social media platforms in the Indian agribusiness sector in addressing challenges arising from the pandemic. These strategies can be adopted by other agribusiness firms to communicate with their stakeholders in a timely and efficient manner, build trust and loyalty, and drive growth during these difficult times.

2.3 Crisis Communication Strategies for Agribusinesses during the COVID-19 Pandemic

The COVID-19 pandemic has created significant disruptions in the global agribusiness sector. In this context, effective crisis communication strategies are paramount for businesses to successfully navigate the challenges and mitigate the impact of the pandemic. This section will explore crisis communication strategies for Indian agribusinesses during the COVID-19 pandemic, along with examples of companies that have implemented these strategies effectively.

One of the critical components of crisis communication is clear and timely communication with stakeholders. Agribusinesses should keep their stakeholders informed about changes in operations, supply chain disruptions, and government regulations and guidelines. To achieve effective communication, agribusinesses can use various communication channels, including social media, websites, email, and phone (Zhang et al., 2020).

Another important aspect of crisis communication is addressing stakeholders' concerns and queries promptly and empathetically. Agribusinesses should be transparent with their stakeholders about the challenges they are facing and the steps they are taking to mitigate the impact. Promptly addressing stakeholders' concerns and queries can build trust and loyalty among customers, suppliers, and employees (Zhang et al., 2020).

Several Indian agribusinesses have implemented effective crisis communication strategies during the COVID-19 pandemic. For example, Mahindra Agri Solutions (MAS), a subsidiary of the Mahindra Group, used various communication channels to inform its stakeholders about the company's operations during the pandemic. MAS created a dedicated helpline and email address for customers to address their concerns and queries promptly. MAS also used social media and its website to inform customers about new products and services and guidelines issued by the government (Mahindra Agri Solutions, 2020).

Similarly, Godrej Agrovet, a diversified agribusiness company, established a crisis management team to manage the impact of the pandemic on the company's operations. Godrej Agrovet used various communication channels, including social media and email, to update its stakeholders about the company's responses to COVID-19. Godrej Agrovet also implemented measures such as work-from-home arrangements and sanitation protocols to ensure the safety of its employees (Godrej Agrovet, 2020).

Effective crisis communication is essential for Indian agribusinesses to mitigate the impact of the COVID-19 pandemic. Clear and timely communication, transparency, and empathy are critical components of crisis communication strategies. Examples from companies such as Mahindra Agri Solutions and Godrej Agrovet demonstrate that companies can successfully implement these strategies to address stakeholders' concerns, maintain trust and loyalty, and drive growth during these challenging times. The COVID-19 pandemic has created significant disruptions in the Indian agribusiness sector. Effective communication is essential for agribusinesses to mitigate the pandemic's impact. Clear and timely communication, transparency, and empathy are critical components of crisis communication strategies. Companies such as Mahindra Agri Solutions and Godrej Agrovet have implemented effective crisis communication strategies during the pandemic. These companies used various communication channels, including social media, email, and phone, to inform stakeholders about the company's operations and respond to their concerns and queries promptly.

Agribusiness must prioritize effective communication to navigate the pandemic successfully. These strategies can help build trust and loyalty among stakeholders, maintain consistent operations, and drive growth during these challenging times. Crisis communication is a crucial aspect of crisis management. According to Wei and Lu (2018), crisis communication is the process by which an organization communicates with its stakeholders during or after a crisis to inform them of the situation, explain the organization's response, and manage the perception of the crisis. Effective crisis communication can help an organization mitigate the damage of a crisis, maintain stakeholder trust, and potentially turn a negative situation into a positive outcome.

In the context of the COVID-19 pandemic, agribusinesses face unprecedented challenges. Agribusinesses must communicate effectively with their stakeholders to manage the pandemic's impact on their operations and mitigate any negative consequences. The appropriate communication channels and messages depend on the specific stakeholder group. For instance, customers may be concerned about the safety of the product or service, while employees may be worried about their job security. Addressing these concerns through clear communication can help agribusinesses maintain stakeholder trust and loyalty. The use of social media in crisis communication has become increasingly important in recent years, as it is a widely used and accessible platform for stakeholders (Coombs & Holladay, 2012). Social media allows organizations to inform and engage with stakeholders quickly and directly. Companies such as Mahindra Agri Solutions and Godrej Agrovet utilized social media to communicate with their stakeholders during the COVID-19 pandemic. By creating dedicated helplines and email addresses, these companies were able to respond promptly to their customers' queries. Additionally, social media enabled these companies to communicate with customers, suppliers, and employees about the steps they were taking to manage the impact of the pandemic.

Agribusinesses must maintain transparency and honesty in their communication, as these qualities are crucial to building and maintaining stakeholder trust (Zhang et al., 2020). When communicating about the impact of the pandemic, agribusinesses should openly address any challenges they are facing and outline steps they are taking to mitigate the impact. By being transparent, agribusinesses can demonstrate their proactive approach and commitment to stakeholders, potentially turning the crisis into an opportunity to build stronger relationships.

Effective crisis communication is essential for agribusinesses to successfully navigate the challenges of the COVID-19 pandemic. Agribusinesses should prioritize clear communication, transparency, and empathy to maintain stakeholder trust and loyalty. Utilizing social media and other appropriate communication channels can help agribusinesses inform their stakeholders promptly and directly. By effectively communicating during the crisis, agribusinesses can turn a negative event into a positive opportunity for growth and strengthen their relationships with their stakeholder groups.

2.4 Government Policies and Agribusiness Communication during the Pandemic: A Critical Analysis

The COVID-19 pandemic has had a significant impact on the global agribusiness sector, leading to disruptions in production, distribution, and supply chains. In response, governments around the world have implemented policies to mitigate the impact of the pandemic on the sector. Effective communication between the government and agribusinesses is crucial to ensure the smooth implementation of these policies and to support the sector's recovery. This paper critically examines the communication strategies and policies adopted by governments to support agribusinesses during the pandemic. Governments have adopted various policies to support the agribusiness sector during the pandemic. For instance, the Indian government announced a $16 billion package that includes measures to support farmers, such as credit facilities, easing of loan repayment terms, and financial aid for crop losses (Nayak, 2020). Similarly, the US government implemented the Coronavirus Food Assistance Program, which is designed to provide direct support to farmers and ranchers who experienced losses due to the pandemic (US Department of Agriculture, 2020).

However, the implementation of these policies relied on effective communication between government agencies and agribusinesses. Governments needed to clearly communicate the eligibility criteria, application procedures, and timelines for these support programs. In some cases, the communication was unclear or inadequate, leading to delays or confusion (Gatto et al., 2020). This could result in missed opportunities for agribusinesses to access these benefits.

Another aspect of government communication with the agribusiness sector during the pandemic is the provision of information on safety measures and protocols. Governments needed to keep agribusinesses informed of the latest health guidelines and protocols to ensure the safety of their employees. In some cases, this information was not adequately communicated or was inconsistent across regions, leading to confusion and increased risk of infection (Elbehri & Tsigas, 2021). Moreover, the communication strategies employed by governments during the pandemic had an impact on the agribusiness sector's perception of the policies. Government communication needed to build trust and confidence in the policies to encourage agribusinesses to participate. In some cases, government communication was perceived as inadequate or conflicting, leading to skepticism and non-compliance (Gatto et al., 2020).

Effective communication between governments and agribusinesses is crucial for the success of policies aimed at mitigating the impact of the COVID-19 pandemic on the sector. Governments need to ensure that their policies and guidelines are clearly communicated, and that information is consistent and accessible to all agribusinesses. They also need to build trust and confidence in their policies through transparent and empathetic communication. With effective communication, governments can support the agribusiness sector's recovery and resilience in the face of the pandemic. A crucial aspect of government policies and agribusiness communication during the pandemic is the role of technology. With physical distancing measures in place, there is a need to adopt virtual communication and transaction methods to ensure continuity in the agribusiness sector. Governments have leveraged technology to provide support and information to agribusinesses. For instance, the Kenyan government launched an e-voucher system that allowed farmers to access subsidized inputs from agro-dealers (Ouma, 2021). Similarly, the Mexican government used a mobile app to disseminate information on market prices and support programs to small-scale farmers (Garcia-Vargas et al., 2020).

However, the adoption of technology in the agribusiness sector has been uneven across regions, with some areas having limited access to internet and digital tools. This digital divide could lead to unequal access to government support and information, affecting the sector's resilience and recovery. Governments need to address this gap by providing infrastructure and training necessary to enable agribusinesses to adopt digital technology. Another challenge is the potential for misinformation and fake news to spread through digital platforms. The dissemination of false information could have serious consequences for public health, the economy, and social stability. Governments need to ensure that the information provided through digital platforms is accurate, verified, and consistent. They also need to work with credible sources such as scientific institutions, industry associations, and NGOs to provide accurate information.

Another crucial aspect of government policies and agribusiness communication during the pandemic is the need for collaboration and coordination. The pandemic has highlighted the interdependence of different actors in the agribusiness sector and the need for effective collaboration to ensure its functioning. Governments need to work with different stakeholders, including farmers, agro-processors, retailers, transporters, and industry associations, to devise policies that respond to the sector's complex challenges. They also need to adopt an inclusive and participatory approach to communicate these policies to the stakeholders. The COVID-19 pandemic has brought unprecedented challenges to the agribusiness sector, requiring governments to devise policies that respond to its complex and dynamic nature. Effective communication between governments and agribusinesses is crucial to ensure the success of these policies. Governments need to ensure that their policies are clear, consistent, and accessible to all agribusinesses through various communication channels, including digital platforms. They also need to build trust and confidence in their policies through transparent and empathetic communication. Moreover, governments need to work with different stakeholders to promote collaboration and coordination, which are essential for the sector's resilience and recovery in the post-pandemic period.

2.5 Digitalization and e-commerce in Agribusiness Communication during COVID-19: Evaluating Effectiveness and Impact

Digitalization and e-commerce have become increasingly important in the agribusiness sector, especially during the COVID-19 pandemic. The measures put in place to prevent the spread of the virus have resulted in disruptions in the supply chain and traditional marketing channels. As a result, many agribusinesses have turned to digital platforms to reach their customers and improve their sales. This article evaluates the effectiveness and impact of digitalization and e-commerce in agribusiness communication during COVID-19.

The rise of e-commerce in agribusiness is not a recent development. The adoption of digital platforms in agriculture began in the early 2000s (Caswell and Fuglie, 2012), and it has grown significantly over the years. However, the COVID-19 pandemic has accelerated the adoption of digital platforms by agribusinesses. Farmers who traditionally relied on physical markets to sell their produce are now turning to digital platforms such as social media, e-commerce sites, and mobile applications to sell their products.

One of the most significant impacts of COVID-19 on agribusiness has been the disruption of the supply chain. With many countries imposing movement restrictions and closing borders, the transportation of farm produce has been challenging. As a result, some farmers have had to dispose of their produce, leading to significant losses. Digitalization and e-commerce have provided an alternative for farmers to sell their produce without relying on physical markets. Agribusinesses that have adopted digital platforms have been able to reach a wider market, including consumers who were previously out of reach.

Moreover, digital platforms have enabled farmers to communicate directly with their customers, providing them with information about the origin, quality, and safety of their products. This transparency has helped build trust between farmers and consumers, leading to increased sales. Customers are more likely to buy from farmers they trust, and digital platforms have helped build this trust by providing customers with more information about the products they purchase.

Digitalization and e-commerce have also helped agribusinesses to overcome the limitations of physical markets. Farmers who sell their produce through traditional channels face challenges such as limited storage space, perishable goods, and weather conditions that can affect the quality of their products. However, digital platforms have enabled farmers to sell their products online, reducing the need for physical storage space. Moreover, farmers can now transport their products in a controlled environment, ensuring that they reach their customers in good condition.

The effectiveness of digitalization and e-commerce in agribusiness communication during COVID-19 can be evaluated based on the increase in online sales for agribusinesses. According to a report by McKinsey & Company (2020), global e-commerce sales grew by 16% in 2020, with online sales representing 19% of all retail sales. This growth indicates that digital platforms have been effective in reaching customers and increasing sales for agribusinesses.

Digitalization and e-commerce have played a significant role in agribusiness communication during COVID-19. The adoption of digital platforms has enabled farmers to reach a wider market, build trust with customers, overcome supply chain disruptions, and reduce the limitations of physical markets. The effectiveness of digitalization and e-commerce can be evaluated based on the increase in online sales for agribusinesses. With the pandemic still ongoing, it is expected that the adoption of digital platforms in agribusiness will continue to grow, leading to increased efficiency and profitability for agribusinesses

2-6 Case Studies on Successful Agribusiness Communication Strategy during the Pandemic: Key Lessons Learned in India and other countries

The COVID-19 pandemic has brought unprecedented challenges to the agribusiness sector, requiring agribusinesses to adopt new communication strategies to reach their customers. In this article, we will discuss some case studies of successful agribusiness communication strategies during the pandemic in India and other countries and draw key lessons that can be helpful for agribusinesses.

India is an agricultural country with a vast majority of the population still living in rural areas. The COVID-19 pandemic has hit the Indian agrarian sector significantly, resulting in supply chain disruptions, farm labor shortages, and market closures. In response to these challenges, agribusinesses in India have adopted new communication strategies to reach their customers. One such example is the use of mobile applications to connect farmers with retailers and consumers. For instance, AgriBazaar, a mobile application for farmers, has enabled farmers to directly sell their produce online to consumers, eliminating intermediaries and reducing the risk of contagion (Basu, 2020).

Another successful agribusiness communication strategy in India during the pandemic has been the use of social media to reach customers. For instance, the Dairy Dozen campaign launched by the Amul Cooperative Dairy Company in April 2020 used social media platforms like Twitter and Facebook to raise awareness and promote their dairy products, such as milk and cheese. The campaign helped the company to maintain a steady supply of dairy products to market and meet the demand of consumers who were stocking up on essential items (Upadhyaya, 2020). Apart from India, agribusinesses in other countries have also implemented successful communication strategies during the pandemic. In the United States, the California Strawberry Commission launched the "Support Local Farms" campaign, which encouraged people to buy from local strawberry growers who were struggling to sell their produce due to the pandemic (California Strawberry Commission, 2020). The campaign utilized social media to create awareness and provided resources for consumers to find and purchase locally grown strawberries.

In Canada, the Ontario Greenhouse Vegetable Growers Association (OGVG) launched the "Buy Local" campaign to support local growers and encourage people to buy fresh vegetables from their local markets or online. The OGVG used various communication channels like social media, email marketing, and influencer partnerships to promote their products and support local businesses (OGVG, 2020). The successful agribusiness communication strategies mentioned above provide some key lessons for agribusinesses during the pandemic. Firstly, agribusinesses need to adopt digital platforms like mobile applications and social media to reach their customers, especially in a scenario where traditional marketing channels are disrupted. Secondly, transparency regarding the source, quality, and safety of products is necessary to build trust with customers. Thirdly, agribusinesses need to adapt to changing circumstances quickly and launch communication campaigns to support local businesses and create awareness among consumers.

The COVID-19 pandemic has transformed the way agribusinesses communicate with their customers. Successful agribusiness communication strategies during the pandemic rely on the adoption of digital platforms, transparency, and quick adaptation to changing circumstances. The COVID-19 pandemic has disrupted the agribusiness sector globally, and farmers have faced challenges in accessing markets, inputs, and labor. Communication strategies have played a critical role in addressing these challenges by providing timely and accurate information to farmers. This subtopic highlights case studies of successful agribusiness communication strategies during the pandemic from India and other countries and identifies key lessons learned.

In India, the International Crops Research Institute for Semi-Arid Tropics (ICRISAT) has implemented an effective communication strategy for farmers during the pandemic (Narayanamoorthy & Nidumolu, 2020). ICRISAT established a helpline that farmers could call to receive information on market prices, weather forecasts, and agricultural practices. The helpline, which was run by trained agricultural scientists and extension personnel, enabled farmers to make informed decisions about their farming activities and access markets for their produce. ICRISAT also utilized social media platforms such as WhatsApp to broadcast messages to a large number of farmers. The messages included information on crop management practices, government schemes, and pest and disease management.

In Nigeria, the Alliance for a Green Revolution in Africa (AGRA) partnered with private sector organizations to deliver critical agribusiness information to farmers during the pandemic (Akinnigbagbe, 2021). AGRA used various communication channels such as radio, mobile phones, and social media to reach farmers in remote areas. The organization provided information on the availability of inputs such as seeds and fertilizers and facilitated the transportation of produce to markets. AGRA also established a database of farmers and agribusiness enterprises who were interested in buying or selling produce, which enabled them to connect with one another and access markets.

In Peru, the Ministry of Agriculture and Irrigation (MINAGRI) used a mobile app to provide information and services to farmers during the pandemic (World Bank, 2020). The app, called Agrorural, allowed farmers to access market prices, weather forecasts, and input suppliers. The app also had a feature that enabled farmers to report crop damage caused by natural disasters, which helped the government to quickly respond to their needs. MINAGRI utilized local radio stations to promote the app and trained extension workers on how to use it.

These case studies highlight several key lessons. First, communication strategies that are tailored to the needs and preferences of farmers are more effective. For example, farmers in remote areas may prefer to receive information through mobile phones or radio rather than social media platforms. Second, partnerships between public and private sector organizations are essential for delivering critical information and services to farmers during crises. Third, technology-enabled platforms such as mobile apps can be effective tools for providing real-time information and services to farmers. Finally, the involvement of trained agricultural scientists and extension workers in communication strategies is crucial for ensuring the authenticity and relevance of the information provided to farmers. Agribusiness communication strategies have played a critical role in addressing the challenges faced by farmers during the COVID-19 pandemic. The case studies from India, Nigeria, and Peru have demonstrated the effectiveness of tailored communication strategies that utilize various channels and partnerships to deliver critical information and services to farmers. These strategies have also highlighted the importance of involving trained agricultural scientists and extension workers in communication efforts. The lessons learned from these case studies can inform the development of effective communication strategies in the agribusiness sector during future crises.

The case studies from India and other countries discussed in this part provide valuable lessons for agribusinesses to navigate the challenges posed by the pandemic and thrive in a digital and socially distanced world.

Appendix

Crisis Communication Plan Template for Agribusinesses

1. Introduction:
    a. Brief description of the company, its mission, and values.
    b. Explanation of the importance of having a crisis communication plan.
    c. Overview of key stakeholders important to Agribusiness, including their information needs and potential reactions.
2. Potential Crisis Events:
    a. List of potential crisis events that might affect Agribusiness, including natural disasters and man-made events.
    b. Evaluation of the severity of each event, its impact on the business, possible response measures, and potential communication strategies.
3. Crisis Communication Team:
    a. Identification of the crisis communication team.
    b. Contact information for each team member.
    c. Roles and responsibilities of each team member.
    d. Guidelines for team meetings and decision-making.
4. Communication Guidelines:

  a. Preferred communication channels for different types of stakeholders.
  b. Template for holding statements for each type of crisis event.
  c. Guidelines for sharing information with the media, including who will serve as the spokesperson.
  d. Social media guidelines for communication.

5. Implementation:
  a. Instructions for implementing the plan.
  b. Timeline and action plan to initiate the crisis communication plan as soon as a crisis event emerges.
  c. Plan for monitoring and evaluating communication during and after the crisis.

6. Continuous Improvement:
  a. Evaluation plan to assess the effectiveness of the crisis communication plan.
  b. Guidelines for revising the plan on a periodic basis based on feedback and evaluation.

This crisis communication plan template for Agribusiness can be used to prepare for potential crisis events, identify key stakeholders, outline communication strategies, and effectively manage communication in the event of a crisis. It can be customized to meet the unique needs of an individual Agribusiness.

Chapter Section Summaries

2-1. Impact of COVID-19 on the Agribusiness Value Chain: Implications for Communication Strategies

This part discusses the effects of the COVID-19 pandemic on the agribusiness value chain, particularly on the production, processing, distribution, and consumption of agricultural products. It highlights the importance of effective communication strategies for agribusinesses to mitigate the impacts of the pandemic, such as supply chain disruptions, changes in consumer demands, and employee safety and health concerns. The part suggests that agribusiness communication should be tailored to the specific needs and challenges of each stage of the value chain, and that digital communication channels should be used to reach stakeholders and customers.

2-2. Leveraging Social Media for Effective Agribusiness Communication during the Pandemic

This part explores the use of social media platforms, such as Facebook, Twitter, and Instagram, for agribusiness communication during the COVID-19 pandemic. It argues that social media can be a powerful tool for reaching and engaging with customers, suppliers, and other stakeholders, and for providing timely and accurate information on the availability, safety, and quality of agricultural products. The part suggests that agribusinesses should develop a social media strategy that is consistent with their brand and values, and that includes regular updates, images, and videos.

2-3. Crisis Communication Strategies for Agribusinesses during the COVID-19 Pandemic

This part discusses the importance of crisis communication strategies for agribusinesses during the COVID-19 pandemic, and provides a framework for developing such strategies. It highlights the need for agribusinesses to be proactive, transparent, and empathetic in their communication with stakeholders, and to provide clear and concise information on the risks, implications, and actions taken in response to the crisis. The part suggests that agribusinesses should also be prepared to respond quickly to emerging issues and to adapt their communication strategies as needed.

2-4. Government Policies and Agribusiness Communication during the Pandemic: A Critical Analysis

This part critically analyzes the role of government policies in shaping agribusiness communication during the COVID-19 pandemic. It examines the policies and interventions adopted by governments around the world to support the agribusiness sector, and discusses the challenges and opportunities these policies present for effective communication with stakeholders. The part suggests that agribusinesses should engage with governments and other stakeholders to shape policy responses that are aligned with their needs and priorities, and that communication strategies should be adapted to reflect the changing policy landscape.

2-5. Digitalization and e-commerce in Agribusiness Communication during COVID-19: Evaluating Effectiveness and Impact

This part evaluates the effectiveness and impact of digitalization and e-commerce in agribusiness communication during the COVID-19 pandemic. It examines the use of digital technologies, such as online marketplaces, mobile apps, and blockchain, for improving the efficiency, transparency, and sustainability of the agribusiness value chain, and discusses the opportunities and challenges these technologies present for communication with stakeholders. The part suggests that agribusiness communication should be integrated with digital platforms and tools, and that strategies should be evaluated regularly to ensure alignment with evolving technological trends.

2-6. Case Study on Successful Agribusiness Communication Strategy during the Pandemic: Key Lessons Learned

This part presents a case study on a successful agribusiness communication strategy during the COVID-19 pandemic, and identifies key lessons learned for other agribusinesses facing similar challenges. The case study describes the communication efforts of a large agribusiness company in addressing supply chain disruptions, employee safety, and changing consumer demands, and highlights the importance of transparency, empathy, and innovation in crisis communication. The part suggests that agribusinesses should learn from successful case studies to develop their own communication strategies, and that continuous evaluation and adaptation are critical for success.

Discussion Questions

1-1 What are the different stages of the agribusiness value chain, and how has COVID-19 impacted each stage?

1-2 How can the use of social media positively impact agribusiness communication during the pandemic?

1-3 Based on your knowledge of effective crisis communication strategies, how would you apply them to agribusinesses during the crisis situation such as COVID-19 pandemic?

1-4 What are the pros and cons of government policies related to agribusiness communication during the pandemic?

1-5 How have digitalization and e-commerce impacted the agribusiness industry during COVID-19, and what is the effectiveness of these strategies on communication?

1-6 Based on the key lessons learned from a successful agribusiness communication strategy during the pandemic, how would you create a communication strategy that is effective for your own hypothetical agribusiness?

Application Cases

Case Study 1: KisanMithra Farmer Producer Company Limited

Introduction:

KisanMithra Farmer Producer Company Limited is a cooperative movement that was established in Kerala to promote sustainable and organic farming practices among its members. It is a unique initiative where farmers come together to form a company and leverage their collective resources for better farming practices. This case study focuses on KisanMithra's communication strategies and how it contributed to the growth of the cooperative and its impact on the local community.

KisanMithra's Communication Strategies:

KisanMithra's communication strategies were a crucial part of its success. The company used various communication channels such as branding, marketing, and public relations to promote its services and products. The company's branding efforts were aimed at creating a unique identity for KisanMithra and positioning it as a sustainable and organic farming company. The company's marketing efforts were aimed at promoting the products produced by its members. This helped the farmers reach a wider audience and sell their products at fair prices. The company used public relations to build relationships with the local community, government agencies, and other stakeholders. This helped the company gain a good reputation and support for its initiatives.

Impact of COVID-19 on the Agribusiness Value Chain:

COVID-19 had a significant impact on the agribusiness value chain. The pandemic disrupted the global food supply chain and resulted in supply chain disruptions, labor shortages, and price fluctuations. The outbreak of COVID-19 led to a sudden increase in demand for organic and sustainable food products. This created an opportunity for KisanMithra to expand its market reach and build brand awareness.

Questions

1. How did KisanMithra use communication strategies to promote its services and products?
2. What was the role of branding in KisanMithra's success?
3. How did KisanMithra leverage marketing to promote its members' products?
4. How did KisanMithra use public relations to build relationships with the local community?
5. What impact did COVID-19 have on the agribusiness value chain and how did KisanMithra respond to this?

Case Study 2: Case Study of IFFCO: Effective Communication Strategies for Empowering Farmers

Introduction

Indian Farmers Fertiliser Cooperative Limited (IFFCO) is a renowned cooperative society that focuses on providing fair prices to farmers, cooperative education, and technical and marketing support to Indian farmers. Founded in 1967, IFFCO is one of the largest fertilizer cooperatives in the world, serving millions of farmers across India and worldwide. This case study explores how IFFCO's communication strategies have helped foster a strong sense of community among farmers and improved their quality of life.

Communication Strategies

IFFCO incorporates various communication strategies to convey its mission and vision to farmers. One such strategy is its use of technology to keep farmers informed of the latest fertilizer products and farming techniques. IFFCO's mobile app, mIFFCO, offers farmers real-time updates on crop prices, weather conditions, organic farming, and other agricultural news. The app has made it easier for farmers to connect with IFFCO experts and seek answers to their farming and fertilizer-related queries.

Another important communication strategy utilized by IFFCO is community outreach programs. The organization has invested in building strong relationships with farmers by conducting workshops, training programs, and other events to educate farmers about organic farming, sustainable practices, and environmental management. Such programs have helped empower farmers and promote sustainable farming practices.

Empowering Farmers

IFFCO's cooperative model helps empower farmers by providing them with access to affordable inputs such as seeds, fertilizers, and pesticides. This model ensures that farmers receive fair prices for their crops and prevent them from being exploited by middlemen. IFFCO's cooperative model also encourages farmers to form self-help groups and promotes collective bargaining power.

Impact on Agriculture

IFFCO has had a significant impact on the Indian agriculture sector. It helps farmers increase their productivity by providing them with access to quality inputs and fertilizers that enhance the growth of crops. The organization also offers training on modern farming techniques that help farmers produce better yields. As a result, IFFCO has contributed to the overall development of the agriculture sector in India.

Conclusion

IFFCO has shown that effective communication strategies can help empower farmers, foster strong relationships with communities, and have a positive impact on the agriculture sector. Agribusinesses can benefit from IFFCO's learnings by adopting similar communication strategies. By safeguarding themselves from potential crises and having effective crisis communication strategies in place, agribusinesses can ensure they have a positive impact on the communities they serve, even during challenging times.

Questions

1. What are some effective communication strategies adopted by IFFCO that can benefit other agribusinesses?
2. How can effective communication strategies help agribusinesses foster strong relationships with communities?
3. What is the impact of effective communication strategies on the agriculture sector and the communities they serve?
4. Why is it important for agribusinesses to safeguard themselves from potential crises and have effective crisis communication strategies in place?
5. What are some key takeaways that agribusinesses can learn from IFFCO's communication strategies to positively impact the communities they serve even during challenging times?

References

AgriBazaar (2020), 'Farm to Fork : Farmer can sell directly the Buyers ', Available at https://www.agribazaar.com/ (Accessed: 2 January 2021).

Akinnigbagbe, O. (2021). Private Sector-led Partnerships Help Farmers Access Inputs and Markets During COVID-19. Alliance for a Green Revolution in Africa. Retrieved from https://agra.org/private-sector-led-partnerships-help-farmers-access-inputs-and-markets-during-covid-19/

Amuedo-Dorantes, C., & Sarzosa, M. (2020). The impact of COVID-19 on the global agricultural supply chain. Applied Economic Perspectives and Policy, aepa. ppaa038.

Basu, S. (2020). Amid lockdown, startups use mobile tech for agri marketing. Retrieved from https://economictimes.indiatimes.com/industry/banking/finance/startups/amid-lockdown-startups-use-mobile-tech-for-agri-marketing/articleshow/75278803.cms

California Strawberry Commission. (2020). Supporting local farms. Retrieved from https://www.californiastrawberries.com/blog/supporting-local-farms/

Cameron, G. T., & Coombs, W. T. (2018). Crisis communication: Trends and future directions. Routledge.

Caswell, M., & Fuglie, K. (2012). The adoption and implementation of agricultural technology: Lessons from the US agricultural innovation system. Handbook of Agricultural Economics, 2, 11-45.

Chowdhury, A., Bose, I., & Maachiswala, S. (2020). Leveraging technology for mitigating agri-supply chain disruptions during COVID-19: Lessons from India. Journal of Agricultural and Food Information, 21(4), 358-368.

Christensen, L. T., & Fan, Y. (2018). Crisis communication in the age of social media: A network perspective on crisis management. In Handbook of research on crisis leadership in organizations (pp. 1-21). Edward Elgar Publishing.

Coombs, W. T., & Holladay, S. J. (2012). The Handbook of Crisis Communication. Blackwell Publishing.

Elbehri, A., & Tsigas, M. E. (2021). COVID-19 and food safety: Risk management and innovations. Applied Economic Perspectives and Policy, 43(1), 156-178.

Fernandez, E. J., & Ruiz, C. (2020). Crisis communication templates. Encyclopedia of Business and Professional Ethics. Springer.

Garcia-Vargas, M., Banuelos-Ruedas, F., Vazquez-Valdez, O., Roman-Roque, B., & Alvarez-Ramirez, J. (2020). The Role of Mobile Technologies in Improving Smallholder Farmers' Access to Markets During COVID-19 Across Different Countries. Frontiers in Sustainable Food Systems, 4, 130.

Gatto, A., Iannotta, M., Wang, H., & Yang, L. (2020). The impact of government responses to COVID-19 on agriculture and food systems. Agricultural Systems, 183, 102873.

Godrej Agrovet (2020). Covid-19 Statement. Available at https://www.godrejagrovet.com/sites/default/files/inline-images/Covid%2019%20Statement.pdf (Accessed: 2 January 2021).

Mahindra Agri Solutions (2020). Ensuring our farmers' safety and well-being during the COVID-19 crisis. Available at https://www.mahindraagrisolutions.com/ensuring-our-farmers-safety-and-wellbeing-during-the-covid-19-crisis/ (Accessed: 2 January 2021).

McKinsey & Company. (2020). COVID-19 and agrifood tech: Accelerating a revolution. Retrieved from https://www.mckinsey.com/industries/agriculture/our-insights/covid-19-and-agrifood-tech-accelerating-a-revolution

Narayanamoorthy, A., & Nidumolu, U. (2020). COVID-19 Response by CGIAR Centers: ICRISAT's Experience. CGIAR. Retrieved from https://www.cgiar.org/news-events/news/covid-19-response-by-cgiar-centers-icrisats-experience/

Nayak, K. (2020). Government aid for agriculture can help the sector remain resilient during COVID-19. World Bank Blogs. Retrieved from https://blogs.worldbank.org/opendata/government-aid-agriculture-can-help-sector-remain-resilient-during-covid-19

Ninjacart (2020), 'Ninjacart | Fresh Products Directly from Farmers', Available at https://www.ninjacart.in/ (Accessed: 2 January 2021).

OGVG. (2020). Buy local campaign. Retrieved from https://ontariogreenhouse.com/news/buy-local-campaign

Ouma, E. (2021). Kenya's Agriculture Ministry opens online shop for e-voucher inputs for subsistence farmers to order remotely. Precision Agriculture for Development: Kenya. Retrieved from https://pad-kenya.org/kenya%E2%80%99s-agriculture-ministry-opens-online-shop-for-e-voucher-inputs-for-subsistence-farmers-to-order-remotely/

Pendell, D. L., McFadden, D. T., Marsh, T. L., & Brester, G. W. (2020). Agribusiness innovations in response to the COVID-19 pandemic. Applied Economic Perspectives and Policy, 43(1), 61-74.

Swinnen, J., Dominguez-Torres, C., & Tamer, G. E. (2020). COVID-19 and global food security. EuroChoices, 19(2), 17-23.

The Packer (2020), 'Dole takes to social media for pandemic updates', 12 May. Available at https://www.thepacker.com/article/dole-takes-social-media-pandemic-updates (Accessed: 2 January 2021).

Tyson Foods (2020), 'A Message to Our Customers About COVID-19', Available at https://www.tysonfoods.com/news/news-releases/2020/4/a-message-to-our-customers-about-covid-19 (Accessed: 2 January 2021).

Upadhyaya, P. (2020). Dairy dozen: How Amul Milk and cheese kept supply steady during Covid-19. Retrieved from https://theprint.in/business/dairy-dozen-how-amul-milk-and-cheese-kept-supply-steady-during-covid-19/429550/

US Department of Agriculture. (2020). Coronavirus food assistance program. Retrieved from https://www.farmers.gov/cfap

Wang, J., Xue, Y., Rao, V. R., & Wei, Q. (2020). Crisis communication strategies and guidelines for agribusinesses during COVID-19. Agribusiness, 36(3), 365-372.

Wei, H., & Lu, Y. (2018). Crisis communication and its impact on brand reputation: a meta-analysis of existing research. Journal of Business Research, 88, 238-246.

World Bank. (2020). Peruvian Farmers Turn to Tech to Adapt to Climate Change During COVID-19. World Bank. Retrieved from https://www.worldbank.org/en/news/feature/2020/09/23/peruvian-farmers-turn-to-tech-to-adapt-to-climate-change-during-covid-19

Zhang, Z., Asante, E., Yoo, J. J., & Li, X. (2020). Exploring communication strategies for enhancing sustainability and resilience of agribusiness during and post COVID-19. Sustainability, 12(21), 8994.

3

Entrepreneurship Skill for Agriculture and Allied Industry Concept: Overview and Importance

Learning Objectives

a) To learn concept and overview of entrepreneurship definition, nature, and characteristics
b) To learn need for and importance of Entrepreneurship in Agriculture and Allied industries
c) Learn benefits of being an entrepreneur in Agriculture sector
d) Get familiar with types of entrepreneurs in Agriculture sector
e) Recommended Skills for Entrepreneurs in Agriculture sector
f) Get overview of the factors affecting entrepreneurial behaviour
g) Overview of Government Promotional schemes for Entrepreneurs in Agriculture sector & noteworthy startups
h) Learn Trends for the Next Three Years (2023-2025)
i) Overview Role of Emerging Technologies in transforming Indian agriculture sector

3.1 Introduction

Entrepreneurship plays a vital role in driving economic growth, and its significance in the agriculture and allied industry cannot be overlooked. As the backbone of many economies, agriculture and its allied sectors provide employment to a significant portion of the global population. In this chapter, we will delve into the concept and overview of entrepreneurship in the context of agriculture and allied industry, exploring its definition, nature, characteristics, and the need for entrepreneurial skills. We will also highlight the benefits of being an entrepreneur in this sector, discuss the different types of entrepreneurs, provide relevant statistics and case studies, and touch upon the factors affecting entrepreneurial behaviour. Additionally, we will examine the current trends and forecast for the next three years in the agricultural entrepreneurship landscape and examine relevant statistics and case studies and shed light on the government's role in promoting entrepreneurship in the Indian startup ecosystem.

But why are we discussing Entrepreneurship skills for Agriculture and allied industries now?

1. Agritech startups have raised over $1 billion in funding in the past 5 years.
2. The Indian agritech market is expected to reach $15 billion by 2025.
3. There are over 1,000 agritech startups in India.
4. The top three agritech sectors in India are precision agriculture, farm management, and farm equipment rental.

3.2 Concept and Overview

Entrepreneurship refers to the process of identifying, creating, and pursuing opportunities to create value by organizing resources effectively. Entrepreneurs are individuals who possess a unique set of skills and mindset, driven by a passion for innovation and a desire to solve real-world problems. They can identify gaps in the market, take calculated risks, and turn ideas into profitable ventures.

In the context of the agriculture and allied industry, entrepreneurial ventures encompass a wide range of activities, such as farming, Agri-processing, Agri-logistics, agricultural equipment manufacturing, and agricultural technology development. These ventures contribute to increased agricultural productivity, improved supply chains, technological advancements, and rural development.

3.3 Definition, Nature, and Characteristics

Agricultural entrepreneurship can be defined as the ability to identify and capitalize on opportunities within the agricultural sector by introducing innovative products, services, and business models. The nature of agricultural entrepreneurship involves understanding the complexities of the industry, including market dynamics, supply chain management, government policies, environmental factors, and technological advancements.

Successful agricultural entrepreneurs possess certain key characteristics such as resilience, adaptability, risk-taking ability, innovation, and a deep understanding of the agricultural ecosystem.

3.4 Need and Importance

The need for entrepreneurship skills in the agriculture and allied industry arises due to several factors. These are, the ever-growing global population demands increased agricultural productivity to ensure food security, there is a need to bridge the gap between urban and rural areas, fostering inclusive growth by promoting rural entrepreneurship, the sector requires innovation and technological advancements to overcome challenges such as climate change, resource scarcity, and sustainability and entrepreneurship in agriculture can create employment opportunities, reducing rural-urban migration and alleviating poverty. Let us examine what makes Indian Agriculture sector unique:

1. **Agricultural Contribution to GDP:** The agriculture sector contributes significantly to India's GDP. According to the Ministry of Statistics and Program Implementation, the agriculture, forestry, and fishing sectors accounted for 17.8% of India's GDP in the fiscal year 2020-21. Source: Ministry of Statistics and Program Implementation www.mospi.gov.in
2. **Employment in Agriculture:** Agriculture remains a major source of employment in India. As per the Periodic Labour Force Survey (PLFS) conducted by the National Sample Survey Office (NSSO), around 42.7% of the country's workforce was engaged in agriculture and allied activities in 2019-20. Source: National Sample Survey Office www.mospi.gov.in
3. **Crop Production:** India is one of the world's largest producers of various crops. As per the Ministry of Agriculture and Farmers Welfare, India produced approximately 292 million metric tons of food grains during the 2020-21 crop year. Source: Ministry of Agriculture and Farmers Welfare www.agricoop.gov.in
4. **Horticulture Production:** India is a significant player in horticulture production as well. According to the National Horticulture Board, the country produced about 326 million metric tons of horticulture crops during 2020-21. Source: National Horticulture Board www.nhb.gov.in
5. **Organic Farming:** The organic farming sector in India has witnessed considerable growth. As per the Agricultural and Processed Food Products Export Development Authority (APEDA), India produced 3.87 million metric tons of certified organic products in 2020-21. Source: Agricultural and Processed Food Products Export Development Authority www.apeda.gov.in
6. **Agri-Exports:** India is a major exporter of agricultural products. The Agricultural and Processed Food Products Export Development Authority (APEDA) reported that the country's agricultural and processed food exports reached $41.25 billion during the financial year 2020-21. Source: Agricultural and Processed Food Products Export Development Authority www.apeda.gov.in

7. **Irrigation Coverage:** Irrigation plays a crucial role in agriculture. The Ministry of Jal Shakti reported that as of March 2021, the total irrigation potential created in India was around 142 million hectares. Source: Ministry of Jal Shakti www.jalshakti-dowr.gov.in
8. **Farmer Producer Organizations (FPOs):** FPOs have gained prominence in recent years, empowering farmers and promoting collective action. The Small Farmers Agri-Business Consortium (SFAC) reported that as of March 2021, there were approximately 10,000 registered FPOs in India. Source: Small Farmers Agri-Business Consortium www.sfacindia.com
9. **Agricultural Credit:** Access to credit is essential for farmers. The National Bank for Agriculture and Rural Development (NABARD) reported that agricultural credit disbursement in India reached Rs 16.02 lakh crore in the financial year 2020-21. Source: National Bank for Agriculture and Rural Development www.nabard.org
10. **Government Agricultural Schemes:** The Indian government has implemented various schemes to support the agriculture sector. One such initiative is the Pradhan Mantri Kisan Samman Nidhi (PM-KISAN) scheme, under which direct income support is provided to eligible farmers. As of May 2023, over 14.6 crore farmers have been benefited under the scheme. Source: Ministry of Agriculture and Farmers Welfare www.agricoop.gov.in

3.5 Benefits of Being an Entrepreneur in Agriculture

Being an entrepreneur in the agriculture and allied industry offers numerous benefits. It allows individuals to be their own boss and pursue their passion for agriculture. It provides the opportunity to make a positive impact on society by addressing food security challenges and promoting sustainable practices. Agricultural entrepreneurship can be financially rewarding, enabling individuals to generate wealth and contribute to economic development. It fosters creativity, innovation, and learning, as entrepreneurs constantly seek new solutions to address the ever-evolving needs of the industry. Being an entrepreneur in the agriculture sector in India offers several benefits, few of them have been listed below.

1. **Income Generation:** Agriculture entrepreneurship provides the opportunity to generate income and create wealth. By implementing innovative practices, diversifying crops, or adopting value-added processes, entrepreneurs can increase their profitability and financial stability.

2. **Job Creation and Rural Development:** Entrepreneurship in agriculture plays a crucial role in job creation, particularly in rural areas. By establishing agribusinesses, entrepreneurs can provide employment opportunities, reducing unemployment and fostering rural development.

3. **Food Security Contribution:** Agricultural entrepreneurs contribute to ensuring food security in India. Through innovative farming techniques, improved supply chain management, and adoption of technologies, entrepreneurs enhance agricultural productivity, leading to increased food production and availability.

4. **Technological Innovation:** Agriculture entrepreneurship encourages the adoption and development of advanced technologies in farming practices. Entrepreneurs can leverage technological advancements, such as precision farming, Internet of Things (IoT), and data analytics, to optimize resource utilization, increase productivity, and improve efficiency.

5. **Market Access and Value Addition:** By establishing agri-processing units, agricultural entrepreneurs can add value to their produce and gain access to wider markets. Value addition through processing, packaging, and branding enables entrepreneurs to fetch higher prices for their products and improve their market competitiveness.

6. **Sustainability and Environmental Impact:** Entrepreneurship in agriculture promotes sustainable practices and environmental stewardship. Through organic farming, water conservation, soil health management, and adoption of eco-friendly practices, entrepreneurs contribute to preserving natural resources, reducing environmental degradation, and promoting sustainable agricultural systems.

7. **Social Impact:** Agricultural entrepreneurship has a significant social impact. By establishing farmer producer organizations (FPOs) or engaging in social entrepreneurship, entrepreneurs can empower farmers, enhance their bargaining power, and improve their socio-economic conditions. Such initiatives contribute to inclusive growth, poverty alleviation, and rural community development.

Above benefits highlight the transformative role of entrepreneurship in the agriculture sector, offering opportunities for economic, social, and environmental advancement in India.

3.6 Types of Entrepreneurs

The agricultural entrepreneurship landscape consists of four types of entrepreneurs.

1. **Traditional Farmers:** There are traditional farmers who venture into agribusiness by diversifying their farming activities and adopting innovative practices.
2. **Agripreneurs:** There are agripreneurs who focus on the development and commercialization of agricultural technologies, such as precision farming, smart irrigation systems, and farm management software.
3. **Social Entrepreneurs:** They play a crucial role in addressing social and environmental challenges in the agricultural sector, creating sustainable and inclusive business models.
4. **Rural Entrepreneurs:** Lastly, there are rural entrepreneurs who establish enterprises in rural areas, providing employment opportunities and contributing to local development.

3.7 Recommended Skills for Indian Entrepreneurs in Agriculture Sector

To be a successful entrepreneur in the agriculture sector in India, it is crucial to possess a diverse set of entrepreneurial skills. 18 skills that are important for aspiring agricultural entrepreneurs are listed below:

1. **Domain Knowledge:** Having a deep understanding of agricultural practices, crop cultivation, livestock management, and related technologies is essential.
2. **Problem-Solving:** Being able to identify challenges and find innovative solutions to address them is crucial in the dynamic agricultural landscape.
3. **Adaptability:** Being open to change, adjusting to market trends, and embracing new technologies and practices are essential for long-term success.
4. **Risk Management:** Understanding and managing risks associated with crop failure, weather uncertainties, market fluctuations, and financial challenges is crucial in the agricultural sector.
5. **Financial Management:** Being adept at managing finances, budgeting, and resource allocation is crucial for sustainable business operations.
6. **Marketing and Sales:** Having the skills to promote agricultural products effectively, identify target markets, and build strong customer relationships is important for business growth.

7. **Networking:** Developing a strong network of industry contacts, suppliers, potential customers, and stakeholders is beneficial for collaborations and accessing market opportunities.
8. **Leadership:** Possessing strong leadership skills to guide and inspire a team, delegate tasks, and make informed decisions is important for managing agricultural enterprises.
9. **Communication:** Effective communication skills are essential for building relationships with stakeholders, negotiating contracts, and conveying ideas and information clearly.
10. **Technical Skills:** Proficiency in using agricultural technologies, farm machinery, software applications, and data analysis tools, digital marketing, no code/low code platforms is beneficial for enhancing productivity and efficiency. Overview of Project Management Practices is must for managing risk and delivery.
11. **Time Management:** Being able to prioritize tasks, manage schedules, and optimize productivity is important in the agricultural sector, where timely operations are critical.
12. **Creativity and Innovation:** Thinking creatively and seeking innovative approaches in farming practices, value addition, and market strategies can give entrepreneurs a competitive edge. Knowledge of design thinking would be beneficial.
13. **Strategic Planning:** Developing a clear vision, setting achievable goals, and formulating long-term strategies are vital for business growth and sustainability.
14. **Resourcefulness:** Being resourceful in utilizing available resources, optimizing inputs, and finding alternative solutions can help overcome challenges in the agriculture sector.
15. **Emotional Intelligence:** Having the ability to understand and manage emotions, empathize with others, and build strong relationships is valuable in agricultural entrepreneurship.
16. **Environmental Awareness:** Being conscious of sustainable farming practices, environmental impact, and biodiversity conservation is important for long-term sustainability.
17. **Quality Management:** Maintaining high standards of quality in agricultural produce, adhering to food safety regulations, and ensuring customer satisfaction are essential for success.
18. **Continuous Learning:** Being open to learning, staying updated with

industry trends, and embracing new knowledge and technologies are crucial for continuous improvement and growth.

These entrepreneurial skills, combined with a passion for agriculture and a strong work ethic, can greatly contribute to success in the agriculture sector in India. Honing these skills would give you an edge over your peers.

3.8 Factors Affecting Entrepreneurial Behaviour

Several factors influence entrepreneurial behaviour in the agriculture and allied industry. Market conditions, access to finance, government policies, technological advancements, and the availability of skilled human resources all play a significant role. Additionally, the level of infrastructure development, the presence of supportive networks and incubation centres, and the cultural and social environment also impact entrepreneurial behaviour in this sector. I have listed nine factors affecting entrepreneurial behaviour in the Indian ecosystem:

1. **Government policies:** The Indian government has been supportive of entrepreneurship in recent years, with policies such as the Startup India initiative. These policies have created a more favourable environment for entrepreneurs, making it easier to start and grow businesses.
2. **Availability of capital:** There is a growing pool of capital available to entrepreneurs in India, from venture capital firms to angel investors. This has made it easier for entrepreneurs to raise the funding they need to start and grow their businesses.
3. **Access to talent:** India has a large pool of talented people, many of whom are graduating from top universities. This has made it easier for entrepreneurs to find the talent they need to build their businesses.
4. **Strong demand for products and services:** The Indian market is large and growing, with a growing middle class that is demanding new products and services. This has created a large market for entrepreneurs to tap into.
5. **Reduced barriers to entry:** The Indian government has been reducing barriers to entry for businesses, making it easier for entrepreneurs to start and operate businesses. This has created a more competitive environment, which has led to innovation and growth.
6. **Growing infrastructure:** India's infrastructure is improving, making it easier for businesses to operate. This includes improvements in roads, railways, airports, and telecommunications.
7. **Rise of technology:** Technology is playing an increasingly important role in the Indian economy, and this is creating new opportunities

for entrepreneurs. For example, technology is being used to improve productivity, reach new markets, and provide new products and services.

8. **Positive attitude towards entrepreneurship:** There is a growing positive attitude towards entrepreneurship in India. This is due to a number of factors, including the success of some high-profile entrepreneurs and the government's support for entrepreneurship. Maintaining momentum and patience are key factors to maintain positive outlook.
9. **Supportive ecosystem:** There is a growing ecosystem of support for entrepreneurs in India, including incubators, accelerators, and mentors. This ecosystem provides entrepreneurs with the resources they need to succeed.

These are just some of the factors that are affecting entrepreneurial behaviour in the Indian ecosystem. The Indian ecosystem is becoming increasingly conducive to entrepreneurship, and this is leading to a growing number of startups and entrepreneurs.

3.9 Government Promotional Schemes and Grants

To foster entrepreneurship in the agriculture and allied industry, governments around the world, including India, have launched various promotional schemes and grants. In India, the government's flagship initiative, the Startup India campaign, offers several benefits, including tax exemptions, easier business regulations, and access to funding. Additionally, the Atal Innovation Mission (AIM) promotes innovation and entrepreneurship among students, including those in the agriculture sector. The Pradhan Mantri Krishi Sinchai Yojana provides financial support for the development of agricultural water resources and efficient water management. Certainly! Here is a list of some prominent government promotional schemes and grants for the agriculture sector in India:

1. **Pradhan Mantri Krishi Sinchayi Yojana (PMKSY):** This scheme aims to enhance water use efficiency in agriculture through various interventions such as micro-irrigation, water harvesting, and watershed development. Website: http://pmksy.gov.in/
2. **Pradhan Mantri Fasal Bima Yojana (PMFBY):** It is an insurance scheme that provides financial support to farmers in case of crop loss due to natural calamities, pests, or diseases. Website: http://pmfby.gov.in/
3. **National Agriculture Market (e-NAM):** This digital platform connects agricultural produce markets across India, enabling farmers to sell their produce online, access transparent price discovery, and expand their market reach. Website: http://enam.gov.in/

4. **Rashtriya Krishi Vikas Yojana (RKVY):** The scheme aims to provide financial assistance to states for agricultural development activities, including infrastructure development, farm mechanization, and promoting agribusiness entrepreneurship. Website: http://rkvy.nic.in/
5. **National Food Security Mission (NFSM):** It focuses on increasing the production and productivity of food grains in targeted districts through interventions such as promoting hybrid seeds, modern farming techniques, and crop diversification. Website: http://nfsm.gov.in/
6. **Paramparagat Krishi Vikas Yojana (PKVY):** This scheme promotes organic farming practices by providing financial assistance to farmers for adopting organic inputs, traditional seed varieties, and organic certification. Website: http://www.paramparagatkrishi.gov.in/
7. **Pradhan Mantri Kisan Samman Nidhi (PM-KISAN):** This scheme provides direct income support of Rs. 6,000 per year to eligible small and marginal farmers in three equal instalments. Website: http://pmkisan.gov.in/
8. **Interest Subvention Scheme for Short-Term Crop Loans:** Under this scheme, farmers receive interest subvention on short-term crop loans, reducing the cost of borrowing and easing the financial burden. Website: http://www.agricoop.nic.in/
9. **Soil Health Card Scheme:** It aims to assess and issue soil health cards to farmers, providing recommendations on nutrient management, improving soil fertility, and optimizing fertilizer use. Website: http://soilhealth.dac.gov.in/
10. **Agriculture Infrastructure Fund (AIF):** This fund provides financial support to develop and strengthen agricultural infrastructure, including primary processing units, cold chains, and post-harvest management infrastructure. Website: http://agriculture.gov.in/
11. **Department of Animal Husbandry and Dairying, Government of India:** This department has various programs benefiting the animal husbandry and dairy sector. These programs can be accessed at https://dahd.nic.in/schemes-programmes.

These are just a few examples of the numerous government schemes and grants available to support the agriculture sector in India. It is advisable to visit the respective government department websites or consult with agricultural extension offices for detailed information on eligibility criteria, application procedures, and specific scheme updates. Alongside, the list of government startup schemes promoting agriculture in India, along with their respective websites is given as under;

1. Atal Innovation Mission (AIM), Website: https://aim.gov.in/
2. Startup India, Website: https://www.startupindia.gov.in/
3. National Agricultural Innovation Fund (NAIF), Website: http://www.naif.org.in/
4. Agritech Startup Scheme (ASTRA), Website: http://www.agritech.mnre.gov.in/
5. Pradhan Mantri Micro Units Development and Refinance Agency Ltd. (MUDRA), Website: https://www.mudra.org.in/
6. National Bank for Agriculture and Rural Development (NABARD) - Agri Business Incubation (ABI) Fund, Website: https://www.nabard.org/
7. Make in India - Food Processing and Agribusiness Sector, Website: https://www.makeinindia.com/
8. Small Farmers Agri-Business Consortium (SFAC), Website: https://www.sfacindia.com/
9. National Innovation Foundation (NIF), Website: https://nif.org.in/
10. Rashtriya Krishi Vikas Yojana (RKVY), Website: http://rkvy.nic.in/

These schemes and initiatives support startup ventures and innovative ideas in the agriculture sector, providing financial assistance, mentoring, networking opportunities, and access to resources. It is advisable to visit the respective websites for detailed information, eligibility criteria, and application procedures related to these startup schemes.

3.10 Noteworthy Startups

According to the Indian Startup Ecosystem Report 2022, the agritech sector in India witnessed significant growth, with over 450 agritech startups emerging between 2014 and 2022. These startups attracted around $1.3 billion in funding, indicating the immense potential and investor interest in the sector. For instance, DeHaat, an agritech startup based in India, provides farmers with end-to-end agricultural solutions, including access to inputs, financial services, and market linkages. The company has impacted the lives of over 500,000 farmers and aims to reach 10 million farmers by 2024. Here are 7 case studies of agritech startups from India in 2023, along with some statistics:

1. **Tata Kisan Sansar** is a farm management platform that helps farmers with everything from crop planning to market access. The company has over 1 million registered users and has helped farmers increase their yields by an average of 20%.

2. **KisanHub** is a marketplace for agricultural products and services. The company connects farmers with buyers, suppliers, and other resources. KisanHub has helped farmers sell their products for a higher price and access better inputs.
3. **ClimateSmart** is a climate-smart agriculture company that helps farmers adapt to climate change. The company provides farmers with weather data, crop insurance, and other resources. ClimateSmart has helped farmers reduce their losses due to climate change by an average of 50%.
4. **CropIn** is a precision agriculture company that helps farmers improve their yields by using data analytics. The company provides farmers with data on soil health, crop health, and weather conditions. CropIn has helped farmers increase their yields by an average of 15%.
5. **Tractor2U** is a farm equipment rental company that provides farmers with access to the latest farm equipment. The company has over 10,000 registered users and has helped farmers save an average of 25% on their farm equipment costs.
6. **Empower Agri** is a farm management software company that helps farmers manage their farms more efficiently. The company's software helps farmers with tasks such as crop planning, record keeping, and financial management. Empower Agri has helped farmers increase their profits by an average of 10%.
7. **FreshR** is a fresh produce supply chain company that helps farmers get their produce to market faster and fresher. The company has a network of over 1,000 farmers and 100 retailers. FreshR has helped farmers increase their sales by an average of 20%.

These are just a few examples of the many agritech startups that are working to improve the lives of farmers in India. These startups are using technology to address some of the biggest challenges facing the agricultural sector, such as climate change, low productivity, and poor access to markets. With continued innovation, agritech startups have the potential to transform the Indian agricultural sector and improve the lives of millions of farmers.

3.11 Trends for the Next Three Years (2023-2025)

Looking ahead, several trends are expected to shape the agricultural entrepreneurship landscape over the next three years. There will be an increased focus on sustainability and climate-smart agriculture, driven by the need to mitigate climate change and conserve natural resources. The adoption of digital technologies, such as Internet of Things (IoT), artificial intelligence (AI), and blockchain, will revolutionize farming practices, enhancing productivity and efficiency. Social entrepreneurship and inclusive business models will gain prominence, aiming to address social and environmental challenges while generating economic value.

These are just some of the ways that technology is transforming agritech startups. With continued innovation, technology has the potential to revolutionize agriculture and help to feed a growing global population. Technology is transforming agritech startups in India and across the globe in a number of ways. Following are some of the key trends to look out for in India in next 3 years:

1. **Precision agriculture:** Precision agriculture uses technology to collect data on soil, crops, and weather conditions. This data can be used to improve crop yields, reduce input costs, and mitigate the effects of climate change. A study by the Food and Agriculture Organization of the United Nations (FAO) found that precision agriculture can increase crop yields by up to 20%.
2. **Farm management software:** Farm management software helps farmers to track their crops, manage their finances, and stay in compliance with regulations. This software can help farmers to improve their efficiency and profitability. A study by the American Farm Bureau Federation found that farm management software can save farmers an average of $10,000 per year.
3. **Agricultural drones:** Agricultural drones can be used to collect data on crops, spray pesticides, and deliver fertilizers. Drones can help farmers to improve their efficiency and reduce their costs. A study by the University of California, Davis found that agricultural drones can reduce the cost of crop spraying by up to 50%.
4. **Robotics:** Robots can be used to perform a variety of tasks on farms, such as harvesting crops, milking cows, and packing produce. Robots can help farmers to reduce their labour costs and improve their productivity. A study by the Massachusetts Institute of Technology (MIT) found that robots can reduce the labour costs on farms by up to 80%.
5. **Artificial intelligence (AI):** AI is being used to develop new technologies for agriculture, such as crop yield prediction, pest and disease detection, and precision irrigation. AI has the potential to revolutionize agriculture and help farmers to produce more food with fewer resources. A study by the McKinsey Global Institute found that AI has the potential to increase global agricultural productivity by up to 20% by 2050.

These are just a few examples of the many studies that have been conducted on the impact of technology on agriculture. These studies show that technology has the potential to revolutionize agriculture and help to feed a growing global population. Unfortunately, not much of statistical research reports are available in Indian context.

3.12 Role of Emerging Technologies in transforming Indian agriculture sector

Several emerging technologies are transforming the agriculture sector in India, revolutionizing farming practices, increasing efficiency, and improving productivity. Here are some key technologies and their impact:

1. Computer Vision
2. Internet of Things
3. Artificial Intelligence
4. Drones & Remote Sensing
5. Blockchain
6. Farm Management Systems
7. Robotics
8. Biotechnology and Gene Engineering
9. Vertical Farming Systems
10. Big Data Analytics
11. Nanotechnology
12. Use of Biometrics and analytics for Animal Health monitoring
13. 5G
14. Renewable Energy Solutions
15. Wifi 6

3.13 Conclusion

Entrepreneurship skills play a crucial role in the agriculture and allied industry, driving innovation, economic growth, and social development. The dynamic and diverse nature of agricultural entrepreneurship offers numerous opportunities for individuals to create value and make a positive impact on society. By leveraging government support, embracing technological advancements, and addressing the challenges of the sector, aspiring entrepreneurs can contribute to sustainable agricultural practices, rural development, and inclusive growth.

As the agricultural landscape evolves, those equipped with entrepreneurial skills will be at the forefront of shaping the future of the industry.

Questions

1. Discuss 5 characteristics of a successful entrepreneur in Agriculture sector.
2. Being an entrepreneur in the agriculture and allied industry offers numerous benefits. Discuss any 5 benefits.
3. Discuss any 5 recommended skills for an entrepreneur in Agriculture and allied industries sector.
4. Discuss 5 factors affecting entrepreneur behaviour.
5. Discuss 5 noteworthy startups in Agriculture and allied industries sector.
6. Discuss benefits of any 5 emerging technologies in Agriculture sector.
7. Provide an overview of any 5 promotional government schemes in agriculture sector.
8. Elaborate 5 trends in Agriculture and allied industries.

References

"Agricultural Entrepreneurship in India: Status, Challenges, and Opportunities," National Institute of Agricultural Extension Management, 2019.

"Atal Innovation Mission," NITI Aayog, https://aim.gov.in/

"Case Study: Farmizen - Connecting Urban Consumers with Farmers," NITI Aayog, https://niti.gov.in/writereaddata/files/writereaddata/CASE_STUDY_ON_FARMIZEN.pdf

India's G20 Presidency. https://static.pib.gov.in/WriteReadData/specificdocs/documents/2023/mar/doc202337167201.pdf

India's G20 Presidency https://static.pib.gov.in/WriteReadData/specificdocs/documents/2023/may/doc2023523202301.pdf

"Indian Startup Ecosystem Report 2021," NASSCOM, 2021.

"National Agricultural Innovation Fund," Indian Council of Agricultural Research, https://www.icar.org.in/national-agricultural-innovation-fund

"Rashtriya Krishi Vikas Yojana," Ministry of Agriculture and Farmers Welfare, http://rkvy.nic.in/

"Startup India: Government Initiative to Promote Entrepreneurship," Invest India, https://www.startupindia.gov.in/

4

Indian Government's Schemes and Incentives for Agriculture & Allied Industry

Learning Objectives

1. Overview of Government schemes and incentives for promotion of entrepreneurship.
2. Overview of Schemes Applicable for Agriculture Startups
3. Focus on Agriculture in G20 countries under India's Presidency in 2023
4. Role of Venture Capital Investments

4.1 Introduction

Despite of pandemic the Indian economy has been growing consistently and Agriculture sector also maintained the momentum. Let us have an overview of investments in India's agritech startups during 2019-2022:

1. Total investment: $2.5 billion
2. Number of deals: 234
3. Average deal size: $10.7 million
4. Top sectors: Market linkage (52%), Farm management (25%) & Agri-inputs (18%)
5. Key drivers of investment: Growing demand for food and agricultural products, Increasing adoption of technology in the agricultural sector and Government support for the agricultural sector

The agritech sector in India has seen significant growth in recent years, with investments increasing by more than 500% in the last three years. This growth is being driven by a number of factors, including:

1. **Growing demand for food and agricultural products:** The Indian population is expected to reach 1.4 billion by 2030, which will put a strain on the country's food supply. Agritech startups are developing solutions

to increase crop yields, improve livestock productivity, and reduce food waste.

2. **Increasing adoption of technology in the agricultural sector:** Farmers are increasingly adopting technology to improve their productivity and efficiency. Agritech startups are developing mobile apps, drones, and other technologies to help farmers with tasks such as crop planning, irrigation, and pest control.
3. **Government support for the agricultural sector:** The Indian government has launched several initiatives to support the agricultural sector, such as the Pradhan Mantri Kisan Samman Nidhi (PM-Kisan) scheme, which provides financial assistance to farmers. These initiatives are creating a favourable environment for agritech startups to operate in.

The agritech sector is still in its early stages of development, but it has the great potential to transform the Indian agricultural sector. With continued investment and support, agritech startups can help to increase food production, improve farmer livelihoods, and make the Indian agricultural sector more sustainable.

4.2 Promotion Schemes for Agriculture

Investment Promotion Schemes plays a crucial role in fostering economic growth, innovation, and job creation. Recognizing its significance, the Indian government has launched several schemes and incentives to promote entrepreneurship across various sectors. These initiatives aim to provide financial support, mentorship, infrastructure, and a conducive ecosystem for startups and aspiring entrepreneurs. In this chapter, we will explore some key government schemes and incentives that are empowering entrepreneurs in India.

1. **Startup India:** Startup India is a flagship initiative launched by the Indian government to nurture and promote startups in the country. It offers a comprehensive support system, including tax benefits, funding opportunities, and simplified regulatory procedures. The initiative also provides a platform for networking, mentorship, and capacity building. Website: https://www.startupindia.gov.in/
2. **Stand-Up India:** Stand-Up India focuses on promoting entrepreneurship among women and individuals from marginalized communities. It provides loans for setting up greenfield enterprises in manufacturing, services, or trading sectors. The scheme aims to encourage inclusive growth and create employment opportunities. Website: https://www.standupmitra.in/
3. **Pradhan Mantri Mudra Yojana (PMMY):** PMMY aims to provide financial assistance to micro and small enterprises through various lending

institutions. It offers three types of loan products - Shishu, Kishore, and Tarun - catering to different stages of business development. The scheme facilitates access to credit for entrepreneurship and promotes self-employment. Website: https://www.mudra.org.in/

4. **Atal Innovation Mission (AIM):** AIM fosters innovation and entrepreneurship by promoting a culture of innovation and providing a platform for startups. It operates through various initiatives, including Atal Incubation Centers, Atal Tinkering Labs, and Atal New India Challenges. AIM supports startups in areas like agriculture, healthcare, education, and clean energy. Website: https://aim.gov.in/

5. **National Small Industries Corporation (NSIC):** NSIC plays a vital role in promoting small-scale industries and supporting the growth of micro and small enterprises. It offers various services such as marketing assistance, technology support, and capacity building programs. NSIC also facilitates access to government procurement opportunities. Website: https://www.nsic.co.in/

6. **Make in India:** Make in India is a campaign that aims to boost manufacturing and promote investment in India. It focuses on creating an investor-friendly environment, improving infrastructure, and simplifying regulatory processes. The campaign encourages startups and entrepreneurs to leverage India's strengths and contribute to the country's growth. Website: https://www.makeinindia.com/

7. **Technology Business Incubator (TBI) Scheme:** The TBI scheme supports the creation and growth of technology-based startups by providing incubation facilities, mentorship, and financial assistance. TBIs act as launchpads for innovative startups and facilitate the commercialization of technology-driven ideas. Website: Varies based on the individual TBIs.

8. **Credit Guarantee Fund Scheme for Micro and Small Enterprises (CGTMSE):** CGTMSE provides collateral-free credit to micro and small enterprises, enabling them to access finance from banks and financial institutions. The scheme encourages lending to startups and small businesses by offering a credit guarantee to the lending institutions. Website: https://www.cgtmse.in/

9. **Women Entrepreneurship Platform (WEP):** WEP aims to empower women entrepreneurs by providing them with a platform for networking, mentorship, and knowledge-sharing. It fosters collaboration among women entrepreneurs, industry experts, and government stakeholders to support and promote women-led businesses. Website: https://www.weibus.in/

10. **National Skill Development Corporation (NSDC):** NSDC works towards skilling and upskilling the Indian workforce, including entrepreneurs, by offering skill development programs and certifications. It collaborates with various training providers to bridge the skill gap and enhance entrepreneurship capabilities. Website: https://www.nsdcindia.org/

11. **National Agricultural Innovation Fund (NAIF):** NAIF provides financial support for innovative projects and startups in the agriculture sector. It aims to encourage research, development, and innovation in agriculture, promoting entrepreneurship and technological advancements. Website: https://www.agriinfra.dac.gov.in/

12. **Department of Animal Husbandry and Dairying, Government of India** has various programs benefiting the farmers and agriculture sector. These programs can be accessed at https://dahd.nic.in/schemes-programmes. Four major programs are highlighted as under;

    a. **Rashtriya Gokul Mission:** Since December 2014, the Rashtriya Gokul Mission (RGM) has been in operation to promote and protect indigenous cattle breeds. The initiative is crucial for increasing milk output and productivity of cows to fulfil the nation's rising milk demand and to increase the profitability of dairy farming for the nation's small-scale farmers. With a budget allocation of Rs. 2400 crore, the initiative is also continued under the umbrella Rashtriya Pashudhan Vikas Yojna from 2021 to 2026. The RGM will lead to increased productivity and programmatic benefits that will spread to all of India's cattle and buffaloes, especially to small and marginal farmers. Since women perform more than 70% of the work involved in raising livestock, this plan will especially benefit women. Website: https://dahd.nic.in/schemes/programmes/rashtriya_gokul_mission

    b. **National Livestock Mission:** The program's emphasis is on entrepreneurial development as well as breed improvement for pigs, sheep, goats, and poultry, including the production of feed and fodder. The three Sub-Missions are used to carry out the scheme. Website: https://dahd.nic.in/schemes/programmes/national_livestock_mission

    i. **Sub-Mission on Breed Development of Livestock & Poultry:** By offering incentives to individuals, FPOs, SHGs, Section 8 companies, and the State Government for entrepreneurship development as well as for breed improvement infrastructure, the sub-mission proposes to sharpen the focus on entrepreneurship development and breed improvement in poultry, sheep, goats, and pigs.

ii. **Sub-Mission on Feed and Fodder development:** This sub-mission intends to promote the supply of certified fodder seeds needed for fodder production and to encourage entrepreneurs to set up fodder blocks, hey bailing operations, and silage making units through financial incentives.

iii. **Sub-Mission on Extension and Innovation:** The sub-mission aims to encourage institutes, universities, organisations, and extension activities, as well as research and development in the fields of sheep, goats, pigs, feed and fodder, and livestock insurance and innovation.

c. **Dairy processing & Infrastructure Development Fund (DIDF):** The DIDF programme aims to upgrade milk processing equipment and facilities and build new infrastructure to process more milk. Following the release of the Union Budget 2017–18, the National Bank for Agriculture and Rural Development (NABARD) has established the Dairy Processing & Infrastructure Development Fund with a corpus of Rs. 8,004 crore. Cattle feed/feed supplement plants, milk transportation (Refer van/insulated tankers, etc.), marketing infrastructure (including e-market system, bulk vending system, parlour, deep freezer, cold storage, etc., commodity and cattle feed go-downs, etc.), and milk transportation system are among the new components to be implemented in June 2021. ICT infrastructure (such as servers, IT solutions, near-real-time devices, and blockchain technology, for example), R&D (laboratory and equipment, new technologies, innovations, and product development, for example), and infrastructure/plants for renewable energy, infrastructure for energy efficiency, Manufacturing facilities for dairy-related pet bottles and packaging materials, as well as a training facility with all of the essential civil and other infrastructure.

d. **Animal Husbandry Infrastructure Development Fund (AHIDF):** The establishment of the Animal Husbandry Infrastructure Development Fund (AHIDF) in accordance with the Atma Nirbhar Bharat Abhiyan stimulus plan has been announced by the honourable prime minister. It has been approved to use the Animal Husbandry Infrastructure Development Fund (AHIDF) to encourage investments from private businesses, MSME, Farmers Producers Organisations (FPOs), and Section 8 companies in order to establish infrastructure for (i) dairy processing and value addition, (ii) meat processing and value addition, and (iii) animal feed plants. The objective of AHIDF include:

i. To help increasing of milk and meat processing capacity and product diversification thereby providing greater access for unorganized rural milk and meat producers to organized milk and meat market.

ii. To make available increased price realization for the producer.

iii. To make available quality milk and meat products for the domestic consumer.

iv. To fulfil the objective of protein enriched quality food requirement of the growing population of the country and prevent malnutrition in children.

v. Develop entrepreneurship and generate employment.

vi. To promote exports and increase the export contribution in the milk and meat sector.

vii. To make available quality concentrated animals feed to the cattle, buffalo, sheep, goat, pig and poultry to provide balanced ration at affordable prices.

13. **National Horticulture Board (NHB):** The National Horticulture Board (NHB), which has its headquarters in Gurugram, was established by the Government of India in 1984 as an autonomous organisation under the administrative supervision of the Ministry of Agriculture and Farmers Welfare. Currently, NHB operates 29 field offices across the nation. The Board's broad goals and objectives include creating production hubs for integrated high-tech commercial horticulture, building post-harvest and cold chain infrastructure, ensuring the availability of high-quality planting materials, and encouraging the use of new tools, technologies, and methods in high-tech commercial horticulture, among other things. Website: https://nhb.gov.in/.

The Indian government's initiatives and schemes for promoting entrepreneurship are instrumental in creating a favourable ecosystem for startups and aspiring entrepreneurs. From financial support to capacity building and mentorship, these schemes provide a comprehensive support system. By leveraging these schemes and incentives, entrepreneurs can realize their ideas, contribute to economic growth, and drive innovation in India.

4.3 Overview of Schemes Applicable for Agriculture Startups

1. **Atal Innovation Mission (AIM):** AIM promotes innovation and entrepreneurship in various sectors, including agriculture. It offers support through initiatives such as Atal Incubation Centers, Atal Tinkering Labs, and Atal New India Challenges.

2. **National Mission for Food Processing (NMFP):** NMFP supports entrepreneurship in the food processing industry by providing financial assistance, infrastructure development, and capacity building programs.
3. **Rashtriya Krishi Vikas Yojana (RKVY):** RKVY aims to enhance agricultural productivity and support entrepreneurship in the agriculture sector through financial assistance for innovative projects and initiatives.
4. **Agritech Startup Scheme (ASTRA):** ASTRA focuses on supporting agri-tech startups by providing financial assistance, incubation support, and mentorship to foster innovation in agriculture.
5. **Startup India:** Startup India offers a comprehensive support system for startups, including those in the agriculture sector. It provides tax benefits, funding opportunities, and simplified regulatory procedures to foster entrepreneurship.
6. **Pradhan Mantri Kisan Sampada Yojana (PMKSY):** PMKSY focuses on enhancing the competitiveness of the food processing industry, which presents opportunities for entrepreneurship and value addition in the agriculture sector.
7. **Pradhan Mantri Krishi Sinchayee Yojana (PMKSY):** PMKSY aims to promote efficient water management in agriculture, creating opportunities for startups that offer innovative solutions for irrigation and water conservation.

4.4 Focus on Agriculture in G20 countries under India's Presidency in 2023

The G20 is an intergovernmental forum that works to address major issues related to the global economy, such as international financial stability, climate change mitigation, and sustainable development. The Agriculture Working Group (AWG) was established in 2011 during the sixth meeting of G20 during the Cannes Summit in France.

During India's G20 Presidency in 2023, the 100th G20 Meeting under India's G20 Presidency, the Meeting of Agricultural Chief Scientists (MACS) was held at Varanasi and concluded successfully in the month of April 2023.

The discussions were focused on various topics such as Innovations and Technological Interventions for Agri-Food Systems Transformation, Frontiers in Science and Technology for Achieving Food Security & Nutrition, Biofortification in Food Crops for Enhancing Nutritional Value, Tropical Seaweed Farming for nutrition and blue growth, Millets And other Ancient Grains International Research Initiative (MAHARISHI), One Health as an

Integrated and Unifying Approach: Partnerships and strategies for coordinated action, Transboundary Pests and Diseases: R&D Priorities for resilient agri-food systems, Climate Resilient Technologies and Innovations for sustainable agri-food systems, Nature-Positive Agriculture: Science and Innovations for building resilient agri-food system, Biological Nitrification Inhibition (BNI): Reducing GHS emissions and increasing crop yields.

Digital Agriculture and Traceability, Digital Technological Solutions for reducing Food Loss and Waste, Agri-tech Startup Ecosystem, Pluralistic Agricultural Extension and Advisory Services (EAS): partnerships for improving lab to land and outreach, Smallholder and Family Farming: G20-Global South Cooperation for Agri-R&D, Public-private Agri-R&D for Public Goods: Experience in Generating and Accelerating Innovations.

The meeting adopted a chair summary cum outcome document focusing on major areas of cooperation in agricultural research and development for food security and nutrition, digital agriculture, resilient agri-food systems and public-private partnership in agricultural R&D. MACS 2023 also supported launching of MAHARISHI which inter-alia will include establishing mechanisms to connect researchers and institutions working on identified grain crops to enhance the dissemination of research findings, identifying research gaps and needs.

Establishing web platforms to connect researchers, exchange data, share communication products and thematic briefs to encourage research and information sharing. Organizing capacity-building activities and international workshops and conferences. Performance identification and recognition to scientists MAHARISHI secretariat shall be housed at Indian Institute of Millets Research (IIMR), Hyderabad with technical support from ICRISAT, One CGIAR Centres and other international organizations.

4.5 Venture Capital Investments

The agriculture sector in India is one of the largest and most important sectors of the economy. It employs over 50% of the workforce and contributes around 17% to the GDP. However, the sector is also facing a number of challenges, including low productivity, high input costs, and inadequate infrastructure.

Venture capitals are typically large firms that invest in early-stage companies with high growth potential. Investment syndicates are groups of investors who pool their capital to invest in a particular company or sector. Angel investors are wealthy individuals who invest in small businesses.

In recent years, there has been a growing interest from venture capitals, investment syndicates and angel investors in investing in the agriculture sector in India. These investors are attracted by the sector's large market size, the potential for high returns, and the need for innovation.

There are a number of factors driving this trend. (a) the Indian population is growing rapidly, and the demand for food is increasing. (b) the government of India is investing heavily in agriculture, with a focus on modernizing the sector and increasing productivity. (c) there is a growing trend of urbanization in India, which is creating new opportunities for agriculture-related businesses.

Investors are investing in a variety of agriculture-related businesses in India, that include.

1. Agri-tech companies that are developing new technologies to improve productivity, such as precision farming and crop protection.
2. Food processing companies that are developing new products and ways to distribute food more efficiently.
3. Logistics companies that are working to improve the efficiency of the supply chain.
4. Financial services companies that are providing loans and other financial services to farmers.

The investments made by venture capitals, investment syndicates and angel investors are helping to drive innovation in the agriculture sector. This is leading to improved productivity, efficiency and profitability, which is benefiting farmers, consumers and the wider economy. Some examples of venture capitals, investment syndicates and angel investors that are investing in the agriculture sector in India would include:

1. Aavishkaar Venture Capital is a venture capital firm that focuses on early-stage investments in the agriculture sector.
2. Kstart is an investment syndicate that invests in early-stage agriculture and food technology companies.
3. AngelList is an online platform that connects angel investors with startups.

These are just a few examples of the many venture capitals, investment syndicates and angel investors that are investing in the agriculture sector in India. The growing trend of investment in the agriculture sector is a positive development for India, as it is helping to drive innovation and improve the productivity and efficiency of the sector. This is benefiting farmers, consumers and the wider economy. Benefits of venture capital, investment syndicates and angel investors investing in the agriculture sector:

1. Increased access to capital: Venture capital, investment syndicates and angel investors can provide much-needed capital to agriculture businesses, which can help them to grow and scale.
2. Access to expertise: Venture capital, investment syndicates and angel investors can provide expertise and guidance to agriculture businesses, which can help them to improve their operations and make better decisions.
3. Network opportunities: Venture capital, investment syndicates and angel investors can provide agriculture businesses with access to a network of other businesses, investors and individuals, which can help them to grow their business.

4.6 Conclusion

Overall, the growing trend of government's promotional schemes, venture capital, investment syndicates and angel investors investing in the agriculture sector is a positive development for India. It is helping to drive innovation, improve productivity and efficiency, and provide much-needed capital to agriculture businesses. This is the decade of transformation, and these investment schemes are acting as a catalyst to the next level of growth for entrepreneurs in Agriculture domain.

Questions

1. Discuss growth of Agriculture and allied industries in last 3 years.
2. Discuss any 5 government promotional schemes for Agriculture sector.
3. Write an essay on National Livestock Mission.
4. Write an essay on Rashtriya Gokul Mission.
5. Write an essay on Dairy processing & Infrastructure Development Fund (DIDF).
6. Write an essay on Animal Husbandry Infrastructure Development Fund (AHIDF).
7. Write brief on 5 government promotional schemes applicable for agriculture startups.
8. Discuss 3 type of agriculture companies that attract investments in India.
9. Discuss 3 benefits of getting venture capital investment for your startup.

References

1st Agriculture Deputies Meeting (ADM) of the Agriculture - Adda247. https://www.adda247.com/upsc-exam/g20-agriculture-deputies-meeting/.

G20 - Agriculture Working Group. https://agricoop.gov.in/awg-g20/

Impact investors flock to startups in agritech - Mint https://www.livemint.com/companies/start-ups/impact-investors-flock-to-startups-in-agritech-11680203735266.html

Investment in Agri tech startups jumps 2-fold to $4.6 bn in FY22 | Mint https://www.livemint.com/companies/start-ups/investment-in-agri-tech-startups-jumps-2-fold-to-4-6-bn-in-fy22-11669834857851.html

The 100th G20 Meeting under India's G20 Presidency, the Meeting of .... https://pib.gov.in/PressReleaseIframePage.aspx?PRID=1917897

The Rise of Agri-tech in India - Invest India https://www.investindia.gov.in/team-india-blogs/rise-agri-tech-india

5

Evolution of the Co-operative Movement Globally and the Role of International Co-operative Alliance

"Co-operatives build a better world" United Nations Organization

Learning Objectives

1. To enable the students gain the basic understanding about Cooperative Society form of organization
2. To understand the evolution and history of Co-operative form of organization
3. To sensitize the students to the progress of Co-operative Movement globally
4. To acquaint the students with International Co-operative Alliance, their role and significance in the development of the Co-operative movement globally

5.1 Evolution of the Co-operative Movement Globally

The Rochdale Society of Equitable Pioneers was founded in Rochdale, England, in 1844 and soon became a prototype for cooperatives worldwide. Its governance structure, known as the Rochdale Principles, is still a key guideline for the design of cooperatives. The social dislocations of the Industrial Revolution inspired workers and enlightened entrepreneurs to establish cooperative societies since the beginning of the nineteenth century.

In 1844, the Rochdale Pioneers, 28 weavers and other artisans, set up their own cooperative society, collected a capital of £1 sterling per member and started a grocery shop called the Rochadale Equitable Pioneers Society, the first Consumer Co-operative Society. The weavers faced miserable working conditions and low wages, and they could not afford the high prices of food and household goods. They decided that by pooling their scarce resources and working together they could access basic goods at a lower price. Initially, there were only four items for sale: flour, oatmeal, sugar and butter. This was the first consumer co-operative which followed a few principles, which laid the foundation of a new form of organization called, " Co-operative Society". By 1850, membership had risen to 600, making the Rochdale Society the first successful cooperative that survived for more than a few years. This inspired others in neighboring cities to start a cooperative according to the Rochdale model. Efforts to establish new cooperatives, to educate cooperators, to lobby for a better legislation for cooperatives, and...

5.2 Guiding Principles of Cooperative as a form or Organization

One of the ways cooperatives differ from other business structures is their adherence to cooperative principles and values that reflect social, political, and business concerns. Cooperatives trace the roots of these principles to the Rochdale pioneers, who established the first modern cooperative in Rochdale, England in 1844. These principles have been refined, adapted, and reinterpreted over time. The seven principles used by the International Cooperative Alliance today are generally accepted by cooperatives worldwide.

Cooperatives are also based on the values of self-help, self-responsibility, democracy, equality, equity, and solidarity. Cooperative members believe in the ethical values of honesty, openness, social responsibility, and caring for others.

1. Voluntary and Open Membership

Cooperatives are voluntary organizations, open to all people able to use their services and willing to accept the responsibilities of membership, without gender, social, racial, political or religious discrimination. The Membership is not restricted based on caste, creed or gender and everyone has an equal opportunity to join the co-operative society as a member.

2. Democratic Member Control

Cooperative societies are democratic organizations. Their affairs should be administered by persons elected or appointed in a manner agreed to by the members and accountable to them. Members of primary societies should enjoy equal rights of voting (one member, one vote). In a public limited company, the number of votes that a shareholder has is dependent on the number of shares and hence the control of the day to day management is with those who have the highest stake. As against that, in Co-operative Societies, irrespective of the capital, One Man – One Vote brings about democratic control.

3. Member Economic Participation

Members contribute equally to, and democratically control, the capital of the cooperative. This benefits members in proportion to the business they conduct with the cooperative rather than on the capital invested. The economic results arising out of the operations of a society belong to the members of that society and should be distributed in such a manner as would avoid one member gaining at the expense of others. This may be done by decision of the members as follows: a) by provision for development of the business of the cooperative; b) by provision of common services; or c) by distribution among the members in proportion to their transactions with the society.

4. Autonomy and Independence

Cooperatives are autonomous, self-help organizations controlled by their members. If the co-op enters into agreement with other organizations or raises capital from external sources, it is done so based on terms, which ensure democratic control, by the members and maintains the cooperative's autonomy.

5. Education, Training and Information

Cooperatives provide education and training for members, elected representatives, managers and employees so they can contribute effectively to the development of their cooperative. Member also inform the general public about the nature and benefits of cooperatives. All cooperative societies should make provision for the education of their members, officers, and employees and of the general public in the principles and techniques of cooperation, both economic and democratic.

6. Cooperation among Cooperatives

Cooperatives serve their members most effectively and strengthen the cooperative movement by working together through local, national, regional and international structures. All cooperative organizations, in order to best serve the interest of their members and their communities, should actively cooperate in every practical way with other cooperatives at local, national, and international levels.

7. Concern for Community

While focusing on member needs, cooperatives work for the sustainable development of communities through policies and programs accepted by the members. The ultimate aim of all cooperatives should be to aid in the participatory definition and the advancement of the common good.

In recognition with these fundamentals, the cooperative members believe in the values such as: honesty, openness, social responsibility and caring for others and major values and self-help, self-responsibility, democracy, equality, equity and solidarity as added ones.

5.3. International Co-operative Alliance – ICA

The International Cooperative Alliance was founded in London, England on 19 August 1895 during the first Cooperative Congress. In attendance were delegates from cooperatives from Argentina, Australia, Belgium, England, Denmark, France, Germany, Holland, India, Italy, Switzerland, Serbia, and the USA. Representatives established the International Cooperative Alliance's aims to provide information, define and defend the Cooperative Principles and develop international trade.

The International Cooperative Alliance unites, represents and serves cooperatives worldwide.

Founded in 1895, it is one of the oldest non-governmental organisations and one of the largest ones measured by the number of people represented: 1 billion cooperative members on the planet. It is the apex body representing cooperatives, which are estimated to be around 3 million worldwide, providing a global voice and forum for knowledge, expertise and co-ordinated action for and about cooperatives. More than 310 organisations from 107 countries are members of the International Cooperative Alliance.

The ICA's members are international and national cooperative organisations from all sectors of the economy, namely agriculture, banking, consumer, fisheries, health, housing, insurance, and industry & services. To implement its activities, the International Cooperative Alliance is organised with a Global Office based in Brussels, four Regional Offices (Africa, Americas, Asia-Pacific, and Europe), eight Global Sectoral Organisations (agriculture, banking, retail, fisheries, health, housing, insurance, and industry & services), and five Committees and Networks (gender, research, law, youth, and development). The staff of the ICA and of its regional and sectoral bodies are based in various locations around the globe and are committed to helping members and the cooperative movement.

In 1992, the International Cooperative Alliance (ICA) and members of the Committee for the Promotion and Advancement of Cooperatives (COPAC), the United Nations General Assembly proclaimed the International Day of Cooperatives by the UN by resolution 47/90 of 16 December 1992. The date of the celebration of the International Day was chosen to coincide with the already existing International Cooperative Alliance (ICA) International Cooperative Day with has been celebrated since 1923. Since that date the global community celebrates United Nations International Day of Cooperatives and ICA's International Cooperative Day on the first Saturday of July. Celebrations of the Day are held at the international, national and local levels around the world.

The achievement in forming the ICA 125 years ago and the continued strength of the cooperative model is a testament of its relevance and contribution and around the world. It has been one of the only international organisations to survive both World War I and World War II. Overcoming all the political differences between its members was difficult, but the ICA survived by staying committed to peace, democracy, and by remaining politically neutral.

New forms and kinds of cooperatives are being invented all the time. Social cooperatives, a noteworthy and impactful experiment in itself, were invented in Italy in the late 1970s, and are now extending all over the world. We have recently seen the emergence of freelancers' cooperatives, community cooperatives, and different types of multi-stakeholder cooperatives around innovative cooperative entrepreneurial models. It is clear that new forms of cooperatives will continue to emerge as the socio-economic needs of human beings evolve and common aspirations manifest into a collective will to build a better world.

5.4 Cooperative Movements in different Countries

Co-operative movement, was well accepted in different countries and here we document its progress in different countries.

1. Great Britain: In Great Britain, Robert Owen (1771-1858) established self-contained semi-agricultural, semi-industrial communities and Dr. William King (1757-1865) helped to spread Owen's doctrine; his ideas were more reasonable than Owen's and achieved more results.

2. India: The cooperative movement in India has begun in the early twentieth century, and then it spread to other Asian and African countries. It also spread into capitalist countries such as the United States of America, Canada, Israel and Australia.

3. Germany: Robert Owen (1771-1858), is generally regarded as the founder of the modern co-operative movement with the workers of Belles, as "doctrine of circumstances". William King (1786-1865) was another pioneer who helped a lot in building up co-operative ideology, published a monthly paper "co-operative" in which he made an education campaign to popularize the co-operative ideology.

   Germany is the birthplace of co-operative Agricultural credit movement in the World. In India, the inspiration for the co-operative movement come largely form Germany. Herr F.W. Raiffeisen and Herr Franz Schulze, helped farmers and laborers, started making experiments with various methods of relief. In 1850, Schulze established his first credit society to raise funds to be lent to its members.

4. Ireland: Farmers are the main beneficiaries of the cooperative movement in Ireland.
5. Israel: The first agricultural collective settlement at Dagania in the Jordan Valley during 1908 is the main cooperative movement.
6. Italy: Luigi Luzzati and second was Dr. Leone Wollemburg Pioneer in co- operative movement, during 1880, concentrated on improving the conditions of the poor people.
7. Sweden: During 1870, the cooperative movement stared in Sweden in industrial sector.
8. Canada: In 1861, the coalminers had started a co-operative store in Novascotia, followed by the 1911, Saskatchewan Elevator Co. in support of the government to set up a Wheat Board for agricultural farmers.
9. Denmark: Credit associations were started in 1850 to solve problems of the credit through a special law.
10. Russia: The first attempts in Russia made during 1864 through organizing when co-operative stores and credit societies
11. Japan: In 1879, the cooperative movement was stated in the form of consumer's cooperatives with the object of cheep the soaring prices.
12. China :Famines, floods, mutual quarrels and Japanese war are the major cause of starting cooperative movement in China. In 1912, the founder of Chinese Republic, Dr. Sun Yet Sen, pioneered the cooperative moment.

5.5 Variation of the Co-operative Form of Organization–Self Help Groups

Nobel Laureate Professor Mohammad Yunus, who brought alive the concept of 'self-help group' as 'Bangladesh Grameen Bank' to solve economic problems in the lives of the poor and the lower strata of society during the 1970s in Bangladesh. We can trace the origin of the concept of SHGs in Bangladesh. Bangladesh has been acknowledged as a pioneer in the field of micro-finance. Dr. Mehmud Yunus, Professor of Economics in Chitgaon University of Bangladesh, was an initiator of an action research project 'Grameen Bank'.

A group of five prospective borrowers who meet regularly with Grameen Bank field managers. Typically, two of the five prospective borrowers were granted loans. If, after a probationary time period, the first two borrowers meet the terms of repayment, then loans were granted to the remaining group members. Peer pressure acted as a replacement for traditional loan collateral. Grameen became an independent bank in 1983; headquartered in Dhaka, Bangladesh, it has more than 2,200 branches in the country. The Grameen model has come to symbolize an efficient means of helping the poor by providing them with opportunities to help themselves. More than 97 percent of Grameen's loan recipients have been women, who were weaving the famous " Dhakka Mulmul Sarees".

Self-help groups for developing countries are a major means of economic empowerment of grassroots people. On the other hand, this concept is not only adopted by the common people but also government and non-governmental organizations around the world understand the importance of self-help groups. During the economic liberalization (1991- 92) in India, self-help groups were given special encouragement and NABARD played a major role in this process. At the same time, self-help groups were used in the implementation of grassroots developmental plans during the Ninth Five Year Plan (1997- 2022).

5.6 Self-Help Groups

Self-Help Groups (SHGs) are informal associations of people who choose to come together to find ways to improve their living conditions. It can be defined as self-governed, peer controlled information group of people with similar socio-economic background and having a desire to collectively perform common purpose. Even though they are NOT Co-operative Society, SHG as an Association works on similar values like a Co-operative.

Thus SHG can become a vehicle of change for the poor and marginalized. SHG rely on the notion of "Self Help" to encourage self-employment and poverty alleviation. SHGs are an integral part of India's social fabric and have played a significant role in empowering individuals, especially women, and promoting socio-economic development at the grassroots level. These groups typically consist of 10 to 20 members who come together voluntarily to address common concerns, pool resources, and support each other in various aspects of life.

Government Support: The Government of India recognizes the significance of SHGs and provides support through various programs and schemes. The National Rural Livelihoods Mission (NRLM), initiated by the Ministry of Rural Development, focuses on empowering rural women through SHGs and provides financial assistance, capacity building, and livelihood opportunities.

Federations and Networks: SHGs often form federations or networks at the village, block, district, or state levels. These larger associations enable collective decision-making, resource pooling, and advocacy for policy changes. They also facilitate the exchange of experiences and best practices among SHGs.

Self-help groups have been successful in transforming lives and fostering inclusive development in India. They have not only empowered individuals but also contributed to poverty reduction, women's empowerment, and sustainable livelihoods. Famous examples include, Shree Mahilla Griha Udyog (Lijjat Papad Brand)

The Self Employed Women's Association (SEWA) is a member-based organization of women workers, with 1.9 million members spread across fourteen Indian states, as well as seven other countries (Afghanistan, Bangladesh, Bhutan, Maldives, Nepal, Pakistan and Sri Lanka). It began its operations as a registered trade union, in the Indian state of Gujarat in 1972. Over the years, it has grown to become one of the largest organizations of informal workers in the world, acting as a powerful agent of empowerment for poor women who are regularly marginalized in both rural and urban contexts.

SEWA hosts a vast network of cooperative-based sister organizations, encompassing a wide variety of different trades, services, areas and objectives. The founder of SEWA is Ela Bhatt, originally the head of the women's wing of the Textile Labor Association (TLA) of Gujarat, who began to assist self-employed and marginalized women in securing some of the benefits that

originally belonged only to unionized laborers. With a developmental approach strongly rooted in Gandhian principles. SEWA has fostered to this day the creation of 106 workers'

cooperatives (belonging to various trades), which have organized 300 000 women with an annual turn-over of, INR 3 billion USD 45 million, as per ILO report, 2018.

5.7. Conclusion

The cooperative movement was stared in England during 19th Century mainly to protect the interest of workers who spread throughout the world. It spread from there to all parts of the world. But, the movement's objectives are differing from one country to the other, depending upon the circumstances. Cooperatives are in all sectors like agriculture, industry and service, to help the members in the form of wages, employment, productivity and marketing facilities. The cooperatives are differ from one perspective to the other like consumer cooperatives (food and other related products), housing cooperatives (shelter), workers cooperatives (decent work), credit cooperatives (savings and credit), agricultural cooperatives (input to agricultural production, pricing and marketing) etc., Today, the cooperative movement is very much successful with widespread inclusive policy.

Case Study I

Crédit Agricole Group – From Agricultural Finance to Universal Banking

Originally conceived to support and develop France's agricultural sector, Crédit Agricole has had to overcome many challenges in the course of its history.

At the end of the 19th century, farmers struggled to obtain suitable loans. The 1884 Act on professional freedom of association authorised the formation of farmers' unions and created an environment conducive to the emergence of suitable organisations: in 1885, a local initiative by **Louis Milcent and Alfred Bouvet** gave birth to **Société de crédit agricole de l'arrondissement de Poligny** in Salins-les-Bains (Jura), the first organisation of its kind.

Alfred Bouvet (1820-1900), a local entrepreneur, and Louis Milcent (1846-1918), a landowner and former legal assistant at France's Conseil d'Etat, got together in 1885 to create the first local agricultural lending bank (caisse locale de crédit agricole) in Salins-les-Bains, which would serve as a prototype. To support small family farms and attract farmers' votes, the Third Republic passed the Act of 5 November 1894 authorising members of farmers' unions to establish local agricultural lending banks for which they would be liable, in keeping with the principle of mutuality. The government drew inspiration from the Salins-les-Bains model. These local banks are the foundation of the institutional "pyramid" erected by Crédit Agricole.

In the 1920s, Crédit Agricole expanded its geographical footprint and made its first forays into new areas of business, extending loans to small rural tradesmen, financing rural electrification in 1923, granting the first home loans to farmers of limited means in 1928, and so on. These various activities helped improve rural quality of life and thus slowed the exodus from rural to urban areas.

However, the Local and Regional Banks did not emerge unscathed from the 1930s crisis. The most exposed were supported by CNCA, which stepped up its supervisory activities. A joint deposit guarantee fund was set up in 1935. Although the Vichy regime strengthened state control over Crédit Agricole, this was only a temporary state of affairs. However, the institution underwent a major financial transformation during the period: Crédit Agricole issued its first five-year notes, funnelling rural savings to the Treasury.

The 1988 Privatisation Act enabled Crédit Agricole's Regional Banks to acquire CNCA, which became a public limited company completely independent from the state. It was listed on the stock market in 2001 under the name Crédit Agricole S.A. This major step forward enabled Crédit Agricole to expand and diversify by acquiring companies in investment banking (Banque Indosuez in

1996) and consumer credit (Sofinco in 1999 and Finaref in 2003). Following the 2003 tie-up with Crédit Lyonnais, various business lines were combined to give birth to Crédit Agricole Corporate and Investment Bank in 2006. Crédit Lyonnais refocused on retail banking and rebranded as LCL in 2005. Asset management subsidiary Amundi was created in 2010 and quickly became the leading player in its sector.

In 2019, Crédit Agricole drew on its history, its universal banking model and its role as the leading financer of the French economy to formulate its raison d'être: "Working every day in the interest of our customers and society".

Case Study II

Friesland Campina – Diary Co-operatives for the farmers by the Farmers

FrieslandCampina is a a Dutch co-operative multinational dairy cooperative which is based in Amersfoort, Netherlands. is one of the largest dairy cooperatives in the world. We have 9,927 member dairy farms and 15,137 member dairy farmers in the Netherlands, Belgium and Germany. Our member dairy farmers are co-owners of the company through the cooperative. Continue reading to find out how exactly this works.

This Dairy cooperative was established in 1871, when farmers realised that they would be stronger if they stood together. This idea fueled the development of FrieslandCampina into the Organization, it is today. . With 15,137 member dairy farmers operating some 9,927 dairy farms all over the Netherlands, Belgium and Germany, as of date.

As a co-operative society, there is a unique structure, which is democratic and every member has a say in the decision-making. The members' council on behalf of the members votes on major and important decisions. Control by or on behalf of the members can also be found in decision-making on the milk money regulations, changes in terms and conditions relating to the supply or quality of the milk, and other important cooperative changes.

The structure:

The cooperative FrieslandCampina U.A. is owned by the member dairy farmers. Members' meetings are held in their district at least twice a year. The member dairy farmers elect representatives from their district who together form a district council. There are 14 districts and 10 district councilors per district. The 140 district council members together also form the members' council of Friesland Campina U.A. Important proposals or decisions by the board require the adoption or approval of the members' council. Each member of the members' council has the right to vote on behalf of the district. The weight of the vote depends on the amount of milk supplied in the district. Members of the members' council have one vote for every ten million kg of milk that their district supplied to the company during the most recent financial year of the cooperative. With these votes, the members of the members' council represent all dairy farmers of the cooperative.

Brief Questions

1. Trace the evolution of the Co-operative form of Organzation from the Rochadale Society of Equitable Pioneers.
2. Explain briefly the seven guiding principles of Co-operative Society
3. Briefly describe the role and significance of International Co-operative Alliance in the co-operative movement
4. Depict the growth of co-operative movement worldwide

References

Growth & Dynamics of Worker Cooperatives, by White et al (1991)
http://dx.doi.org/10.1002/9780470674871.wbespm055
https://ucanr.edu/sites/sfp/files/143837.pdf
https://www.credit-agricole.com/en/group/history-of-the-credit-agricole-group
https://www.frieslandcampina.com/owned-by-farmers/the-cooperative/
https://www.ica.coop/en
https://www.researchgate.net/publication/334126375_Co-operative_movement
https://www.rfilc.org/library/grameen-bank-groups-and-self-help-groups-what-are-the-differences/
https://www.souharda.coop/pdf/2020/New04.pdf
Industrial Democracy & Workers Owned Firms, Carl Bellas (1972)
Review of International Co-operation Volume 106/2021
Success Factors of New Generation Cooperatives, Carlberg J et al
Survey of Research in Industrial Sociology, Sharit K. Bhowmik (2002)
Sustainable Economic Democracy: Workers Cooperatives for 21st Century, by Nicholas Luviene et al
The Economic Empowerment of Women: The Case of Working Women, S Nachiappan (2008)
The Promise & Problems of Worker Cooperatives, by Carla Dickestein
Women Cooperatives for Medicinal and Innovative Nutritional Plants, Sweta Patel & Sapovadia (2004)

6

Co-operatives in India

"At the heart of all that civilization has meant and developed is 'community' - the mutually cooperative and voluntary venture of man to assume a semblance of responsibility for his brother."

~ Martin Luther King, Jr.

Learning Objectives

- To sensitize the students to Indian culture and co-operation;
- Understand the Co-operative Movement before Independence;
- Evolution of the Co-operative Movement with the Establishment of Credit Co-operative;
- Know the Co-operative Legislation in India before and after Independence;
- Explain the different types of Co-operative in India
- Explain the concept of Self Help Group (SHG)
- Illustrate the Role of Co-operative in Agriculture and Rural Development in Maharashtra

6.1 Evolution of Co-oeprative Movement in India and Maharastra

एकमेका साह्य करू अवधे धरू सुपंथ

- जगद्गुरू संत तुकाराम

Let's support each other and support each other

- Jagadguru Sant Tukaram.

Co-operation and Mutual trust, are some of the most cherished values, as given by the Ancient Indian wisdom and is part of our Indian culture. There is a saying, "Many hands make light work." It is only through mutual trust, cooperation and team spirit can there be all round progress and prosperity, and success for everyone concerned due to the synergistic effects of combined efforts.

6.1.a Co-operation and Indian Culture

Co-operation and Mutual trust, are some of the most cherished values, as given by the Ancient Indian wisdom and is part of our Indian culture. Even before formal cooperative structures came into being through the passing of a law, the practice of the concept of cooperation and cooperative activities were prevalent in several parts of India. Village communities collectively creating permanent assets like village tanks or village forests called Devarai or Vanarai.

Instances of pooling of resources, by various groups like foodgrains similarly, instances of pooling of resources by groups, to lend to the needy members food grains after harvest Collecting small contributions in cash at regular intervals to lend to members of the group viz., Chit Funds and Bhishi Similarly the bunds were built for the equitable distribution of water. Farmers also entered into partnership so that, the lands was cultivated jointly.

6.1.b Establishment of Credit Co-operatives in India before India's Independence

Before India's independence, there was indeed a significant lack of institutional credit available to farmers in the country. The British colonial rule, which lasted for nearly two centuries until 1947, implemented policies that favored large landowners and commercial agriculture at the expense of small-scale farmers.

During this period, the agricultural sector in India predominantly consisted of small and marginal farmers who faced numerous challenges, including limited access to formal credit. The British administration primarily focused on revenue collection rather than investing in rural development or providing financial support to farmers.

Here are some key factors contributing to the lack of institutional credit for farmers in pre-independence India:

Zamindari System: The British introduced the zamindari system, where intermediaries called zamindars were given the rights to collect revenue from peasants on behalf of the colonial administration. This system led to exploitative practices, with zamindars charging exorbitant rates and usurping farmers' profits, leaving them with little capital to invest in their own farms.

Absence of Agricultural Banks: The establishment of formal agricultural banks was minimal during the colonial period. The British administration primarily focused on setting up commercial banks that catered to the needs of urban centers and the colonial administration. As a result, farmers had limited access to financial institutions and relied heavily on moneylenders who charged high interest rates.

Moneylender Dominance: Moneylenders played a significant role in providing credit to farmers in the absence of institutional support. However, they exploited the dire financial situations of farmers, charging exorbitant interest rates and often resorting to unfair practices in debt recovery.

Lack of Agricultural Extension Services: Agricultural extension services, which provide technical advice and support to farmers, were inadequate during the colonial period. The absence of such services further limited the farmers' ability to adopt modern farming techniques, leading to low productivity and financial constraints.

Neglect of Rural Infrastructure: The British colonial administration invested more in urban infrastructure development, focusing on railways, industries, and trading centers. Rural areas, where agriculture thrived, were neglected, resulting in a lack of irrigation facilities, storage facilities, and access to markets. This further hindered the farmers' ability to improve their productivity and economic conditions.

The lack of institutional credit severely affected farmers, perpetuating a cycle of poverty and debt. It was only after India gained independence in 1947 that steps were taken to address these issues and provide adequate institutional credit and support to farmers through initiatives like cooperative banks, rural development programs, and agricultural extension services.

6.2 Co-operative Legislation in India

6.2.a Co-operative Credit Societies Act

The Cooperative Credit Societies Act, 1904, was introduced in British India to regulate and facilitate the formation and functioning of cooperative credit societies. The act aimed to address the issues of rural credit and provide financial assistance to small farmers and agriculturists. Under this act, cooperative credit societies were formed with the objective of providing affordable credit and other financial services to their members. These societies operated on the principle of mutual cooperation and were owned and controlled by their members.

The key provisions of the Cooperative Credit Societies Act, 1904, included

Formation and registration: The act outlined the procedures for forming and registering cooperative credit societies. It defined the eligibility criteria for membership and the minimum number of members required to form a society.

Management and governance: The act prescribed rules regarding the management and governance of cooperative credit societies. It specified the roles and responsibilities of the members, the board of directors, and the committee. It also addressed matters related to elections, meetings, and the conduct of society affairs.

Powers and functions: The act conferred certain powers and functions upon cooperative credit societies. They could accept deposits, raise funds through share capital, borrow money, and provide loans and other financial assistance to their members. The act also allowed them to undertake allied activities, such as providing insurance services and promoting savings habits.

Audit and supervision: The act mandated regular auditing of the accounts and operations of cooperative credit societies. It provided for the appointment of auditors to examine the financial records and submit reports. Government authorities were empowered to supervise and inspect the societies to ensure compliance with the act.

6.2.b The Cooperative Credit Societies Act, 1904

The Cooperative Credit Societies Act, 1904, was later repealed and replaced by subsequent legislation as cooperative movements evolved and expanded. However, cooperative credit societies continue to operate in many countries worldwide, including India, with the objective of empowering rural communities and promoting financial inclusion. \

The First Incorporation Taking cognizance of these developments and to provide a legal basis for cooperative societies, the Edward Law Committee with Mr. Nicholson as one of the members was appointed by the Government to examine and recommend a course of action. The Cooperative Societies Bill, based on the recommendations of this Committee, was enacted on 25th March, 1904. The Cooperative Societies Act was enacted in 1904, which provided a legal framework for the registration, functioning, and governance of cooperative societies. This act paved the way for the formalization and expansion of the cooperative movement across India.

As its name suggests, the Cooperative Credit Societies Act was restricted to credit cooperatives. By 1911, there were 5,300 societies in existence with a membership of over 3 lakhs. The first Cooperative Law of India The Cooperative Credit Societies Act, 1904 was passed on 25th March 1904. Agricultural Credit Cooperative Society, of Kanaginahal village of Gadag District in Karnataka was the first cooperative Society formed under First Cooperative law of India. This was launched on 8th July 1905 by the villagers of Kanaginahal under the leadership of Shri Siddanagowda SannaRamanagaowda Patil with the initial share capital of Rupees two thousand.

6.2.c All India Rural Credit Survey (1954)

The All India Rural Credit Survey conducted in 1954 highlighted the importance of cooperatives in providing credit to farmers. The survey emphasized the need for cooperative credit institutions to cater to the agricultural sector and recommended the expansion of the cooperative movement.

6.3 Formation of Apex Co-operatives Organizations in India

6.3.a Formation of National Cooperative Development Corporation (1963)

The National Cooperative Development Corporation (NCDC) was established in 1963 to provide financial assistance and promote the development of cooperatives in India. NCDC plays a crucial role in providing loans, grants, and technical support to cooperative societies across various sectors.

6.3.b Formation of National Cooperative Union of India (1961)

The National Cooperative Union of India (NCUI) was formed in 1961 as an apex organization to represent and promote the interests of cooperative societies in India. NCUI acts as a platform for cooperation, coordination, and advocacy on behalf of cooperatives at the national and international levels. In India, the cooperative movement gained momentum in the early 20th century. Some notable figures associated with the cooperative movement in India include Sir Frederick Nicholson, Vithalrao Krishnaji Vandekar, Laxmanrao Inamdar, and Vallabhbhai Patel. These individuals played crucial roles in promoting and organizing cooperative societies in various sectors, such as agriculture, credit, dairy, and consumer goods.

6.4 Types of Co-operative Society in India

6.4.a Consumer Cooperative Societys

These societies are primarily for consumers who wish to buy household goods at lower prices. The society buys goods or products in bulk amounts directly from the producer on wholesale rates and sells them to the members, thus eliminating the need for a middleman. The purchased goods are sold to members and non-members in cash. Capital is raised by issuing low denominational shares to the members who also get dividends on the shares. Consumer co-operatives do not use advertising but rely on word-of-mouth. They ensure a regular supply of goods at reasonable rates. They set up stores or outlets to sell goods and avail huge trade discounts from producers. Some of the best examples of a consumer co-operative society are **Apna Bazar and Super Bazar.**

6.4.b Producer Cooperative Society

Also known as industrial co-operatives, these types of cooperative societies look out for the small-scale producers in a cut-throat market scenario. Production and distribution are handled from within the co-operative. These producers could be farmers, ayurvedic herbal medicine producers, organic produce sellers, handicraft or handloom producers, artisans, etc. Raw materials, ingredients, tools, processing units, etc. needed for the manufacturing or producing the goods are obtained by the members directly, provided to the producers and the final output is distributed to the buyers/non-members without a middle link. Producers pool in their resources, increase production volumes and minimise risk in the face of the competitive capitalistic markets. Best examples are dairy, fish farmers, weavers and artisans and tribal co-operatives. One of the famous example is **SEWA – Self Employed Women's Association.**

6.4.c Cooperative Credit Societies

These are urban and rural financial societies that provide loans to members at low rates of interest, protecting the members from massive debts to traditional moneylending agencies. They serve a basic but highly personalised banking role in a sense. They have deposit schemes in forms of saving accounts, FD, RD, pension schemes, etc. The money procured is then given on loans to members as personal loans, agricultural loans, housing or vehicle loan, etc. These societies are regularly aided by state and national government subsidies and funding. Some examples are **Kokani Kunbi Sahakari Pat Pedhi.**

6.4.d Marketing Cooperative Society

Mostly for the benefit of farmers, these societies function to market the produce profitably at the best possible prices, increase the bargaining strength of the farmers and protect them from the trials of individual selling and market exploitation. The profits are distributed on the basis of the contribution of produce made. They also educate the farmers on market prices, stabilise supply against demand, help them get loans, and help with grading, pooling, processing and procurement of produce and provide safe storage and reliable transportation facilities. Some good examples are **Varna Bazar, Kolhapur Zilla Sahakari Dudh Utpadak Sangh Ltd, well known with its popular brand 'Gokul'**

6.4.e Housing Cooperative Society

Housing co-ops are a type of society that provides affordable housing to the middle and low-income groups. One becomes a member by purchasing shares in the cooperative. Instead of owning the real estate, the members own a share in the entire corporation, which in turn gives them a house to reside in. Such societies are commonly found in urban and semi-urban cities. They construct the residences or flats and provide them to the members to live in and collect the money in instalments. In other cases, they provide the land to the members who themselves construct their own residences.

6.4.f Sugar Co-operatives

Maharashtra, a state in India, is known for its significant presence in the sugar industry. The cooperative movement has played a vital role in the development of sugar production in Maharashtra. Sugar cooperatives are agricultural cooperatives formed by farmers to collectively engage in the cultivation of sugarcane and the production of sugar. These cooperatives aim to provide support, infrastructure, and marketing assistance to farmers involved in sugarcane cultivation.

One of the most prominent sugar cooperatives in Maharashtra is the Maharashtra State Cooperative Sugar Factories Federation Ltd (MSCSFF). It is an apex organization representing various cooperative sugar factories in the state. MSCSFF works towards the development and welfare of sugar cooperatives, ensuring the fair pricing of sugarcane, facilitating access to credit, and promoting sustainable practices in the sugar industry. The sugar cooperatives in Maharashtra have significantly contributed to the state's rural economy by providing employment opportunities, supporting farmers' livelihoods, and contributing to the overall growth of the sugar industry in the region. These sugar cooperatives not only focus on sugar production but also engage in activities like ethanol production, power generation from sugarcane by-products, and the manufacture of other value-added products.

Some of the prominent sugar cooperatives in Maharashtra include :

1. Sahakar Maharshi Shankarrao Mohite-Patil Sahakari Sakhar Karkhana Ltd.
2. Maharashtra Rajya Sahakari Sakhar Karkhana Sangh Ltd.
3. Shri Chhatrapati Shivaji Sahakari Sakhar Karkhana Ltd.
4. Kolhapur Sugar Mills Ltd.
5. Vasantdada Patil Sahakari Sakhar Karkhana Ltd.
6. Rajarambapu Sahakari Sakhar Karkhana Ltd.
7. Dhule District Co-operative Sugar Mills Ltd.
8. Pandurang Sahakari Sakhar Karkhana Ltd.
9. Vitthalrao Shinde Sahakari Sakhar Karkhana Ltd.
10. Walwa Cooperative Sugar Factory Ltd.

6.4.g Primary Agriculture Credit Societies (PACS)

Primary Agriculture Credit Societies (PACS) in Maharashtra, India play a crucial role in providing financial assistance and support to farmers and agricultural activities at the grassroots level. PACS are cooperative institutions that aim to uplift the agricultural sector by providing credit and other related services to farmers. They are at the lowest rung of the pyramid, the Apex body being the NABARD and the State Co-operative Bank – Maharashtra State Co-operative Bank. It is a basic unit and smallest co-operative credit institutions in India. It works on the grassroots level (gram panchayat and village level). 2022 put the number of PACS at 1.02 lakh. At the end of March 2021, only 47,297 of them were in profit. Out o the total number of PACS in India, according to the RBI Report, of 1.03 lakhs, at the end of March 2021, only 47,297 of them were in profit.

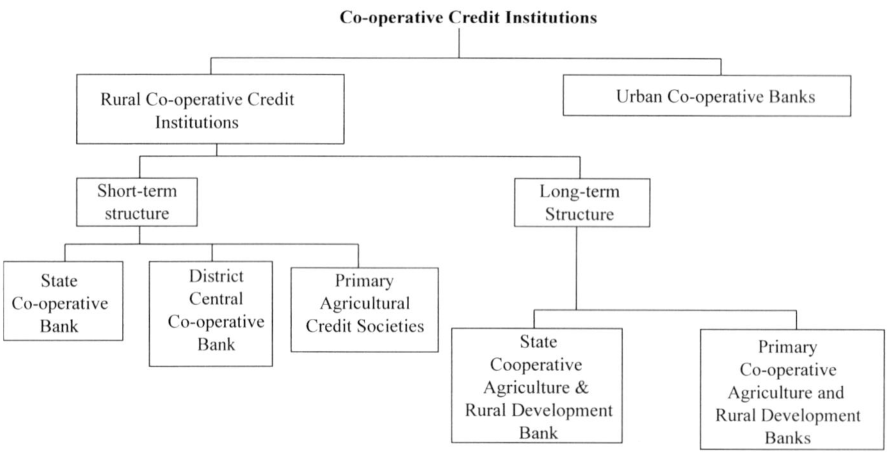

Source: RBI A report published by the Reserve Bank of India on December 27, 2022

6.4.h. Co-operative banks

Co-operative banks : are a specific type of cooperative institution that operates in the financial sector. As cooperatives, they are owned and controlled by their members who are typically the depositors and borrowers of the bank. These banks are guided by the principles and values of the cooperative movement, which prioritize democratic governance, member participation, and mutual assistance. Some of the features of the co-operative banks:

Ownership and control: Co-operative banks are owned and controlled by their members. Each member typically has one vote, regardless of the amount of his or her savings or shares in the bank. The principle of "one member, one vote" ensures democratic decision-making.

Customer focus: Co-operative banks primarily serve their members, who are both the customers and owners of the bank. The banks aim to meet the financial needs of their members and the community rather than maximizing profits for external shareholders.

Social objectives: Co-operative banks often have social and community-oriented objectives. They aim to promote financial inclusion, support local economic development, and provide access to banking services for individuals and businesses that may face difficulties in accessing mainstream financial institutions.

Mutual assistance: Co-operative banks emphasize mutual assistance among their members. They strive to support members' financial well-being by providing affordable credit, savings facilities, and other financial services. The profits generated by the bank are often reinvested to benefit the members and the community rather than distributed to external shareholders.

Local focus: Many co-operative banks have a strong local or regional focus, serving specific communities or regions. They often have a deep understanding of the local needs and are more responsive to the requirements of their members.

Regulatory framework: Co-operative banks are subject to banking regulations and supervision, similar to other types of financial institutions. The specific regulatory framework varies by country and depends on the local laws governing cooperatives and banking activities.

Co-operative banks play an important role in providing banking services and promoting financial inclusion in many countries. They offer an alternative model of banking that prioritizes member needs, democratic decision-making, and community development. Some of the famous Co-operative Apna Sahakari Bank, Kokan Mercantile Co-operative Bank.

6.4.i. Indian Farmers Fertilizer Cooperative Limited

Indian Farmers Fertilizer Cooperative Limited, also known as **IFFCO,** is a multi-state cooperative society. IFFCO is wholly owned by Cooperative Societies of India. The society is engaged in the business of manufacturing and marketing of fertilizers. IFFCO's headquarters are in New Delhi, India. It started its operation in 1967 with 57 member cooperatives; it is today the biggest co-op in the world by turnover on GDP per capita, as per World Cooperative Monitor 2021, with around 35,000 member cooperatives reaching over 50 million Indian farmers. With around 19% market share in urea and around 31% market share in complex fertilizers, P2O5 terms IFFCO is India's largest fertilizer manufacturer. The cooperative was ranked 66th on the Fortune India 500 list of India's biggest corporations as of 2017, with a net worth of $2.6 billion as on March, 2021.

6.5 Role of Co-operative in Agriculture and Rural Development in Maharashtra

Cooperatives play a crucial role in agriculture and rural development in Maharashtra, a state known for its agricultural productivity. The cooperative movement of Maharashtra has made a significant contribution to the economic and social development of rural areas. Here are some key roles and contributions of cooperatives in agriculture and rural development in Maharashtra:

Credit and Finance: Agricultural cooperatives, such as cooperative banks and credit societies, provide financial services to farmers. They offer credit facilities for agricultural inputs, equipment, and working capital. Cooperatives ensure that farmers have access to affordable credit, reducing their dependence on moneylenders and improving their financial stability.

Marketing and Distribution: Agricultural cooperatives help farmers in the marketing and distribution of their produce. They aggregate the produce of small and marginal farmers, enabling collective bargaining power and better market access. Cooperatives often establish storage facilities, processing units, and marketing channels to ensure fair prices and reduce post-harvest losses.

Input Supply: Cooperatives in Maharashtra play a vital role in providing quality agricultural inputs like seeds, fertilizers, pesticides, and machinery to farmers at reasonable prices. By procuring inputs in bulk and eliminating middlemen, cooperatives help reduce input costs and ensure availability of genuine and affordable inputs.

Irrigation and Water Management: Cooperative societies also undertake initiatives for irrigation development and water management. They facilitate the construction and maintenance of irrigation structures, such as canals, reservoirs, and wells, which benefit farmers by providing them with a reliable water supply for irrigation purposes.

Skill Development and Training: Cooperatives organize training programs and workshops to enhance the knowledge and skills of farmers. These initiatives cover various aspects of modern farming techniques, crop diversification, pest management, and use of technology. Skill development programs empower farmers to adopt efficient and sustainable agricultural practices.

Social Welfare: Cooperatives promote social welfare activities in rural areas. They support initiatives related to education, healthcare, women empowerment, and rural infrastructure development. Cooperatives often prioritize the welfare of their members and work towards improving their overall quality of life.

Empowerment and Collective Decision-Making: By encouraging farmer participation and democratic decision-making, cooperatives empower farmers and give them a voice in policy formulation and implementation. They provide a platform for farmers to come together, share experiences, and collectively address their issues and concerns.

The Government of Maharashtra has been actively promoting and supporting the cooperative sector through policies, incentives, and institutional frameworks. The state has various cooperative institutions, such as Maharashtra State Cooperative Bank (MSC Bank), Maharashtra State Cooperative Marketing Federation (MAHAFED), and Maharashtra State Cooperative Cotton Growers Marketing Federation (MAHACOT). These institutions work towards the growth and development of cooperatives in agriculture and rural sectors, ensuring sustainable livelihoods for farmers and overall rural prosperity.

Case Studies: I Rural Empowerment through Co-operatives – Warana Nagar

Shree Tatyasaheb Kore Warana Sahakari Sakhar Karkhana Ltd., (Warana Sugar Co-Operativ})) "Shree Tatyasaheb Kore Warana Sahakari Sakhar Karkhana Ltd." (Warana Sugar Co-Operative), Waranangar, Dist. Kolhapur, a renowned co-operative sugar factory in India promoted by late Tatyasaheb Kore, the Founder and Great Visionary Leader of Co-operative movement in the western part of India, proposes to add some more project activities of Co-generation power project, BNG Gas Plant and Bio-Fertilizer Plant etc., out of waste material and waste water to overcome the environmental issues. The Warana Sugar Co-Operative Industries is the Mother Institution for the other warana Co-Operatives. Covering 110 villages, spread across 25,000 kilometre area with 50,000 farmer members of the society.

The sugar cane factory, which produces 110,000 tons of sugar per year, employs 8,000 workers and collects sugar cane from about 35,000 farmers, is the main source of income for the Warana community. Warana Cooperative Complex is hub of economic activities like, a dairy unit, a food-processing unit, a chain of department stores, poultry farming,and a series of women's co-operatives. The dairy employs 1,200 workers and collects 280,000 litres of milk per day from the 125 milk societies belonging to the dairy co-operative. The dairy co-operative, in turn, provides a series of services to its members;from veterinary aid to cattle shed design, from insemination to subsidy on animal purchases.

Highlights

Daily capacity of approximately 100 tons, or 35,000 annual tons, of sugarcane waste (press mud).

Daily production of approximately 8000 kg's of Bio-CNG per day.

Daily production of approximately 75 tons of organic fertilizer per day.

Substantial cost savings due to low-cost Bio-CNG use Climate friendly – CO2 negative: Biogas-to-CNG conversation is the most productive use of agricultural waste Biogas Projects.

The Warana Co-operative Complex was a forerunner of integrated rural development involving the cooperative movement that has had a classic ingredient of success—peoples participation. The Warana Co-operative Sugar factory initiated this movement that has resulted in the formation of over 55 cooperative societies related to sugar, milk, and poultry production. The total annual turnover of these societies exceeds $1.5 million (approximately Rs 6.5crores). Most of the societies are located within a radius of 4 kilometers. The complex has its own EPABX (Electronic Private Automatic Branch Exchange) facility for voice communication between various centers and societies. Some of the societies such as sugar and dairy have computerized their routine operations.

The sugar factory is the backbone of the Warana complex. The sugar factory has won several awards for its efficiency and productivity. The Warana paper mill was set up to utilize the waste products of the sugar factory. A distillery has also been set up in the complex. An electricity generation unit has been set up using the waste water of the paper mill and the distillery. The energy generated by the unit is used by the paper mill. The Warana complex is designed to look after all the basic needs of the workers. They have been provided with living quarters, filtered water, inexpensive electricity, schools, physical training and cultural centers.

Warana Group consist of more than 55 organizations out of which some major organizations are as under:

1. Shree Tatyasaheb Kore Warana Sahakari Sakhar Karkhana Ltd. (Warana Sugar Co-Operative)
2. Shree Warana Sahakari Doodh Utpadak Prakriya Sangh Ltd. Tatyasaheb Kore Nagar (Warana Dairy, Milk processing Co-Operative)
3. Shri Warana Vibhag Shikshan Mandal Warananagar (Group of Educational Institutions)
4. Surajya Foundation.(NGO)
5. Mahatma Gandhi Medical Trust
6. Shree Warana Sahakari Bank Ltd.
7. Shree Warana Vibhag Sahakari Grahak Mandal Ltd., Warananagar (Warana co-operative Bazaar)

8. Shree Warana Bhagini Mandal (Micro/small Scale women Industries)
9. Shree Tatyasaheb Kore Warana Vibhag Sheti-poorak, Sheti Prashikshan Sahakari Sanstha Ltd., Warananagar (Warana co-operative Farm development, Supply & Training)
10. Wired Village project

Warana Group is engaged in providing various facilities / benefits to the society people. In fact, farmers were suffering at the hands of unpredictable market forces during the period of 1950's. But over a period of time with the emergence of above institutions, the socio-economic scenario have been changed and the members of the family of farmers – son, daughter and wife have been employed in Mahila Udyog, and sugar factories and allied activities and the overall standard of living is improved in the course of time.

Case Studies : II Co-operative Farming – Gambhira Farming Co-operative near Anand

The 60-year-old farming co-operative near Anand has improved members' socio-economic condition.

At a time when not many farming co-operatives are operational in Gujarat that pool resources to till farming land, harvest crops and share benefits, Gambhira farming co-operative near Anand sets an example. The co-operative, which is more than six decades old, has boosted income for 291 member farmers and improved their socioeconomic condition. Sales of crops rose from Rs90,660 in 1953-54 to Rs3.26 cr in 2010-11, states a working paper by NT Sudarshan Naidu.

The paper titled *Co-operative Farming: A Case Study of the Gambhira Collective Farming Society* mentions that agriculture by small farmers is being rendered increasingly unviable owing to downsizing of land holdings, inept resource deployment, farmers' low investment capabilities and the adverse effects of terms of trade. The paper states that the income obtained by each member whose labour contribution amounted to only 150-180 days per year was significantly higher than cultivating individually. It states, on an average, each member received about Rs90,000 (including bonus) in 2009-10.

Income generated from the society has helped the members in multiple ways. They have constructed houses, upgraded their previous ones, and some members have brought land outside the society. Their children receive an education, occasionally with the society's assistance, and at least one member of each family is employed with a government or private enterprise, states the paper.

Gambhira farming co-operative has members from Gambhira, Kothiakhad, Nani-Serdi and Bilpad villages located on Mahisagar River, around 45 km from Anand. In view of the farmers' plight, the government in 1951, distributed 201 acres of land on the riverbed to 176 farmers individually, states the paper.

All members of the society have been divided into 30 working groups for operational convenience. Each group has eight to 14 members, who choose their group leader, and is allocated 13 to 24 acres (average 17 acres).

The Gambhira cooperative created with this rationale in 1953 has successfully overcome the problems associated with unviable holdings by means of collective action, says the paper. The 291 members have been collectively cultivating an area of 526 acres.

The land and other assets belong to the society and the members, individually, do not have ownership rights either on assets or cultivation decisions. The society undertakes primary tillage, purchase of inputs, irrigation and marketing of produce," states the paper.

Collective Farming Society formed in 1953 has successfully overcome the problems associated with small holder farming and the tragedy of commons. The 291 members of the Gambhira Collective have been continuously collectively cultivating an area of 526 acres from 1953 by forming 30 groups of eight to 14 members each. The land and other assets belong to the collective society and the members, individually, do not have ownership rights either on assets or cultivation decisions. The Managing Committee of the collective decides the crop plan to be implemented by respective groups under their group leaders who also happen to be members of these groups. The society undertakes primary tillage, purchase of inputs, irrigation and marketing of produce. The proceeds obtained from crop production from the land allotted to groups, after meeting all the expenses and contribution towards reserve and development fund, is passed on to the respective group leaders who, in turn, share it with group members in proportion to their labour contribution. Group members received higher returns by achieving economies of scale, influencing the terms of trade and optimal utilization of resources. Improved incomes have led to members' improved status in society. The collective has overcome free riding, shirking, and opportunism by forming small groups, devising proper mechanisms for sharing work and profits, monitoring and sanctioning of stakeholders at all levels and institutionalizing rules, norms and values. The Gambhira experiment has proved that collectives can overcome problems faced by farmers who cultivate individually. The collective has overcome the problems of resource constraint and escaped the vicious cycle of low investment-low productivity-low return. Gambhira has proved that the co-operative approach can turn farming into a viable and profitable proposition.

Brief Questions

1. Describe the evolution of Co-operative Movement in India
2. Describe the success stories of Co-operatives in Maharashtra
3. What are the laws, which govern the co-operative societies in India?
4. Explain the role of Rural Empowerment through Co-operatives in Maharashtra
5. What is the role of Primary Agrciltural Co-operatives in credit creation for the farmers?

References

Bhosale S.S. (ed 1982) Pudharikar Gorav Granth, Amrut Mahotsavi Prakashan, Pudhari, Kolhapur.

C.B. Memoria and G. S. Kamat, co-operation : Theory and Practice, 1975, p. 34.

C.B. Memoria and R.D. Saksena, Co-operation in India, Fourth Edn., 1973, p. 121.

Co-operative Movement Centenary Year and Newspaper Coverage. Available from: https://www.researchgate.net/publication/348758993

Dubashi P.R. (1970). Principles and Philosophy of Cooperation, VAMNICOM, Pune.

Hajela, T.N., (2010). Cooperation: Principles, Problems and Practice, Konark Publishing, House, New Delhi

Jadhav Shivaji [2007] Padmashree Late Dr. G.G. Jadhav yanchi Patrakarita, unpublished thesis, pp.182-183

John Winfred A. and Kulandaiswamy V. (1986). History of Cooperative Thought, Rainbow Publications, Coimbatore.

K.A. Abdul Kuddus & Dr. A.K. ZakirHussain, "Theory Law and Practice of Cooperative Banking" Limra Publications

Krishnaswami O.R. (1989). Fundamentals of Cooperation, S. Chand & Co., New Delhi.

Krishnaswami O.R., and Kulandaiswamy, V. (1992). Theory of Cooperation: An Indepth Analysis, Shanma Publications, Coimbatore

N. Rath, and A. K. Mitra, Artha Vijnan (Journal of Gokhale Institute of Politics & Economics), Vol. XXXI, No.l, March, 1989, P. 49.

Patil Pratap (1996). Public relations of Cooperative Societies of Maharashtra, Jaydutt Publication, Kolhapur

R.D. Bedi, Theory, History and Practice of Co-operation, Tenth Edn., 1977, p. 194-95.

Ravichandran, Kand Nakkiran, S. (2009). Cooperation: Theory and Practice, Abijit Publications, Delhi.

Saradha, V. (1986). Theory of Cooperation, Himalaya Publishing House, Mumbai.

T. N. Hajela, Principles, Problems and Practice of 1978, p. 54.

V. Sharada, The Theory of Co-operation, 1986, p. 4-5.